Directing the Agile Organisation

A lean approach to business management

Directing the Agile Organisation

A lean approach to business management

EVAN LEYBOURN

IT Governance Publishing

IT Governance Publishing
IT Governance Limited
Unit 3, Clive Court
Bartholomew's Walk
Cambridgeshire Business Park
Ely
Cambridgeshire
CB7 4EA
United Kingdom

www.itgovernance.co.uk

First published in the United Kingdom in 2013.
by IT Governance Publishing.
ISBN 978-1-84928-491-2

ABOUT THE AUTHOR

Evan Leybourn is an internationally renowned leader, coach and speaker in the developing field of Agile Business Management. He has held executive, board and advisory positions in private industry and government, and worked with clients developing lean business practices across Australia, South East Asia, Europe and America.

Evan has a passion for building effective and productive organisations, filled with actively engaged staff and satisfied customers. His background in Agile project management and business intelligence has informed his understanding of the need for evidence-based decision making, and quantitative analysis to measure corporate success.

Evan currently calls Melbourne, Australia, home.

ABOUT THE CASE STUDY AUTHORS

Chris Moore is the Chief Information Officer at the City of Edmonton. In his role as CIO, Chris provides vision and leadership over the City's information and technology direction. Recognised by *Venture* Magazine as one of Alberta's 50 most influential people, and a founding member of the WeGo (World E-government) organisation, Chris has been described as transformational, innovative, disruptive and refreshing.

Paul Reid is the Group GM Innovation and Strategy at New Zealand Post Limited. He is also an independent director of Software Education (training company), Maven International (consulting) and Chairman of Localist Limited (digital trading platform). Paul is a true, innovative thinker who challenges all the business norms. Previously, Paul has held senior roles in Air New Zealand, Carter Holt Harvey and Ernst & Young.

Thushara Wijewardena is a software professional who has gained over 12 years' experience in managing software project portfolios in various organisational settings. During the last five years, she has put lots of focus on using Agile concepts in offshore-onshore project engagements, as well as implementing Agile at the enterprise level. Thushara is a speaker at leading international conferences, and an author of many articles related to the subject. Currently she works as the Chief Project Officer of Exilesoft.

Dr David Socha is an Assistant Professor in the Computing and Software Systems Program at the University of Washington, Bothell. His research and teaching interests focus on how professional software developers collaborate and design complex software systems, and the design of tools, principles and practices to enable effective software development.

Dr Tyler Folsom is a professional engineer with 30 years of experience. He has published over 40 papers and technical reports. Dr Folsom is a project manager with Qi2, specialising in robotics and machine vision. His current interest is enabling the transition to sustainable transportation based on automated vehicles.

Joe Justice is the CEO of WIKISPEED, leading a global, volunteer network of individuals' intent on bringing a 100mpg (2.25L/100km) car to market, while transforming automotive production.

Adam Spencer is a technology executive with international banking experience and success in program delivery, IT service management, risk management and innovation. His experience includes finance, vendor management, security, agile and leadership of large multinational teams at companies, such as Standard Chartered Bank, KPMG and Suncorp.

Phil Wang is the Executive Audit Manager in the Suncorp Group. With qualifications in technology and business administration, his experiences include the delivery of company-wide technology projects, and the provision of consulting, risk management and assurance services across finance, defence, mining and infrastructure industries.

CONVENTIONS USED IN THIS BOOK

Throughout this book, I have used specific styles and icons to draw your attention to term definitions, tips, examples and case studies. Watch for the following:

 Quotations are used at the beginning of each chapter and section to provide context and invoke thought.

Term definition: These are new, or specific, terms that relate to Agile, or Agile Business Management. These terms will always appear capitalised in the main body of the book. A complete list of terms and definitions can be found in the glossary.

Tips will provide helpful advice, suggestions or caveats to help implement Agile Business Management.

 Examples: Each example illustrates the possible uses of the methods, techniques or processes described in the section.

Case study: A case study is a detailed account of how actual organisations have used these methods. Each case study examines the drivers for change, the solution and its implementation, and the ultimate outcomes. In many cases, the case studies are written by, and attributed to, the reference organisation.

ACKNOWLEDGEMENTS

The seeds of this book started in Canberra, Australia, when, as a software engineer, I first discovered this 'new-fangled' idea called Agile, and loved the focus on rapid, iterative delivery. Later, as a team leader and project manager, I came to appreciate the close engagement with the Customer and related workflow management processes. It wasn't until I started managing companies, and later as a director in the Australian Public Service, that I realised that Agile could go further. Existing processes were inefficient, decisions were made at the wrong level, and nobody seemed to get what they needed, when they needed it. Agile had already solved those problems and could do it again.

This book would not have been possible without the support and assistance of the Agile community. First and foremost, those pioneers in the field who provided the foundational principles on which Agile Business Management has grown. While there are too many to list here, I have referenced them throughout the book, where possible.

I especially thank Thushara Wijewardena, Chris Moore, Ashley Casovan, Paul Reid, Adam Spencer, Phil Wang and the WIKISPEED team, for sharing their deep insights, and providing case studies on the use of Agile in a corporate and non-ICT context. They are true pioneers in this field, and provided much inspiration for writing this book.

Special thanks go out to Srinivas Chillara, Steve Ash and Alexei Zheglov for their early feedback, and help shaping many of the Agile Business Management concepts. These people took time out of their busy schedules to help me through writer's block, point me at new references, and keep the book focused on topic.

Thanks also go to PC.de (*http://pc.de/icons/*) for their lovely Dortmund icons (CC-BY) used in this book. I also want to thank all the people at IT Governance Publishing for all their professionalism and help in getting this book from manuscript to finished product, not forgetting the reviewers: Brian Johnson, CA and Antonio Velasco, CEO, Sinersys Technologies.

I would like to thank my friends, colleagues, and, most importantly, my partner, Nilmini, for their ongoing support and encouragement. Without them, I would have given up on this book a long time ago.

Finally, I dedicate this book to my young daughter, Priyanka Anne Leybourn. My hope is that you grow up in a time where you, and all your generation, are empowered to change the world.

TTFN

Evan Leybourn

April 2013

www.theagiledirector.com

CONTENTS

Contents

INTRODUCTION

'There is nothing wrong in change, if it is in the right direction. To improve is to change, so to be perfect is to change often.'

Winston Churchill, 1925

Agile is about change; changing how you think, changing how you work, and changing the way you interact. By accepting, embracing, and shaping change, you can take advantage of new opportunities to outperform, and out-compete, in the market. While this sounds simple, change, by its very nature, is not easy.

The concepts in this book change what it means to do business. 'Agile Business Management' is a series of concepts and processes for the day-to-day management of your organisation, regardless of industry, size or location. The end goal is to improve business adaptability, staff engagement, quality, and risk management, for the benefit of your Customers.

Agile Business Management is not a quick win; it is not a 'three-step plan' to a 'better business'. Agile Business Management is hard work, and requires a cultural shift from the traditional business practices of hierarchical corporate structures, customer engagement, staff management, and work processes.

This book divides Agile Business Management into four domains, each requiring corresponding changes to the way your business operates. The first domain is You, the Agile Manager. Though it may seem daunting, changing the mindset and processes of management is probably the easiest change to make. It only requires an open mind and a willingness to adapt to a changing business environment.

The second domain is Integrated Customer Engagement – the changing relationship and interactions between you and your Customer. Under Agile Business Management, Customers take on direct responsibility for the delivery of their Requirements. Teams and Customers work closely together, collaborating towards the desired outcomes. To be Agile, means to be flexible and adaptable to changing circumstances, and nothing changes more than your Customer's needs.

The third domain is the Structure of an Agile Organisation – how you manage your staff, the heart of your business, and how they relate to the rest of the organisation. This is a change from a traditional hierarchy, towards self-empowered individuals and Teams. One of the strengths of Agile Business Management is the focus on personal empowerment, developing engaged staff as a mechanism to drive improved customer outcomes. Whilst empowerment is difficult to define and measure, the outcomes are clear. Employees have the responsibility, accountability *and authority* to deliver to the Customer's Requirements.

Having examined the role of the Customer and Team, it's time for the fourth and final domain – Work, the Agile Way. Agile Business Management uses Just-In-Time planning, and an Incremental, or Continuous, Delivery process, that allows for rapid change when scope and circumstances change. Customers work alongside the Team to shape and direct the outcomes, while the Team regularly deliver partial, though functional, products to the Customer.

The product itself will continue to evolve, as each Iteration builds upon the last.

As no two organisations are the same, the design of Agile Business Management is both generic and customisable. Designed to be applicable to most organisations, it is agnostic to the size, industry, nature, location, product base, and culture of your organisation. Where possible, this book also uses common terms and definitions. This means that you will gain the greatest benefit from a considered and tailored implementation, rather than applying every concept in this book verbatim.

There are two approaches you can take when implementing Agile Business Management – the first is a selective, methodical and Incremental approach, and the second is a faster, all-at-once, big-bang approach. While each organisation has different needs, experience shows that a slower, more considered approach to process improvement, usually leads to better results. Start by changing those processes that provide the greatest organisational improvement, observe the outcome, and use that feedback to shape the next change. This is, in itself, an agile approach to Agile. Done correctly, changes in process lead to observable business improvement, which in turn leads to change in the mindset of the organisation. As always, appropriate staff and executive training should complement any organisational change.

Agile Business Management has been many years in the making, and draws on the underlying principles and concepts of the Agile movement. Originally developed by the software engineering industry, you can apply most of the concepts of Agile to technical and non-technical organisations of any size. The management concepts and processes have been implemented across numerous organisations and departments, from managing people and resources, operations management, financial management, Sales and Marketing processes, IT support, and of course software engineering.

Join us for the journey.

What is Agile?

⊂⊃ 'Plans are worthless, but planning is everything.'

Dwight Eisenhower, 1957

Firstly, it is important to understand that Agile is a value system – not a process.

Based on the Lean Manufacturing[1] practices, and adapted and extended for the software industry, Agile is a generic term that describes over 50, sometimes conflicting, methods and frameworks for working in an adaptable, Customer focused, and Incremental way. These frameworks cover the full spectrum of business and product delivery; including strategy, planning, design, development, Q/A and management. Though Agile has only recently gained popular awareness, many organisations have been using these frameworks for over 20 years, and, in the case of lean manufacturing, over 50 years. Well-known Agile frameworks and techniques include Scrum[2], Extreme

---

1 *The Machine That Changed the World,* Womack, Jones and Roos (1991).

2 Scrum Alliance, Scrum, n.d.

Programming (XP)[3], Test-Driven Development (TDD)[4], and Kanban[5].

 Customer: An individual (or organisation) who engages one or more Teams to deliver a series of Requirements, and who has the responsibility, and authority, to direct the delivery of the products or services.

 Team: A small group of between five and nine staff, containing a cross-section of skills, permanently, or temporarily, grouped together to deliver one or more Customer's Requirements.

The first major milestone in the Agile story was in February 2001, when representatives from many of the fledgling Agile processes, such as Scrum, DSDM, and XP came together to write the *'Agile Software Development Manifesto'*[6]. Consisting of four core values and 12 principles, the Agile Manifesto forms the basis of all Agile frameworks, including Agile Business Management, and defines what it means to be 'Agile'.

In Agile Business Management, the four core values define how you do business as an Agile organisation:

1 We value **individuals and interactions** over processes and tools (*see Chapter 3: The Structure of an Agile Organisation*).

---

3 *Extreme Programming Explained: Embrace Change,* Beck (1999).

4 *Test-Driven Development by Example,* Beck (2002).

5 Kanban: Successful Evolutionary Change for Your Technology Business, Anderson (2010).

6 *Agile Manifesto,* Beedle, et al, n.d.

That is, while processes and tools can help sustain a consistent level of output, motivated individuals and Teams collaborating and working together, are more creative, and can produce higher quality work.

2 We value **working software** over comprehensive documentation (*see Chapter 4: Work, the Agile Way*).

In an Agile Business Management context, replace 'working software' with 'delivered Customer Requirements'. This means that, while processes that support delivery are important, the Team's focus should be on delivering to the Customer's needs.

3 We value **customer collaboration** over contract negotiation (*see Chapter 2: Integrated Customer Engagement*).

Written contracts are still important. However, you should be treating your Customer as a partner, not as an opponent. The goal of an Agile contract is to facilitate rather than protect, though it can do that as well.

4 We value **responding to change** over following a plan (*see Chapter 4: Work, the Agile Way*).

Under Agile Business Management, plans are useful as a guide, but adapting to the Customer's changing Requirements brings greater business value, for both you and your Customer.

The values on the right (processes, documentation, contracts and plans) are still important to a successful business; however, to be adaptable and Agile, you need a greater appreciation of the values on the left (individuals, working software, customer collaboration, responding to change).

📋 **Requirement**: Also called a User Story, or Minimal Marketable Feature, a Requirement is a specific, documented and deliverable Customer need.

Supporting the four core values, are the 12 principles of the Agile manifesto that define the Agile mindset. These are the key business attributes that are most important to Agile practitioners. Keep in mind that, although originally written in the context of software engineering, the same mindset applies to business management. The adoption of this mindset within the management structure of an organisation is critical to the success of any Agile Business Management transformation process.

1 Our highest priority is to satisfy the customer through early and continuous delivery of valuable software [Requirements].

2 Welcome changing requirements, even late in development. Agile processes harness change for the customer's competitive advantage.

3 Deliver working software [completed Requirements] frequently, from a couple of weeks to a couple of months, with a preference to the shorter time-scale.

4 Business people and developers [Team Members] must work together daily.

5 Build projects [Teams] around motivated individuals. Give them the environment and support they need, and trust them to get the job done.

6 The most efficient and effective method of conveying information to and within a development Team is face-to-face conversation.

7 Working software [completed Requirements] is the primary measure of progress.

8 Agile processes promote sustainable development. The sponsors, developers [Team Members], and users should be able to maintain a constant pace indefinitely.

9 Continuous attention to technical [and non-technical] excellence and good design enhances agility.

10 Simplicity, the art of maximising the amount of work not done, is essential.

11 The best architectures, requirements, and designs emerge from self-organising Teams.

12 At regular intervals, the Team reflects on how to become more effective, then tunes and adjusts its behaviour accordingly.

Understanding these 12 principles is critical to understanding Agile, and Agile Business Management.

The values and principles of the Agile manifesto, as well as some of the successful Agile frameworks from the ICT industry, form the basis of Agile Business Management. The specific frameworks that Agile Business Management utilises include Scrum (for its Incremental product development processes), Kanban (for its continuous workflow management process), Test-Driven Development (as a mechanism to embed quality control in the work cycle), Feature Driven Development (as a mechanism to break large Customer Requirements into deliverable Tasks) and Extreme Programming (to provide sustainable delivery within Teams).

Scrum

Scrum is described as a 'framework within which you can employ various processes and techniques', rather than a process, or a technique, for building products[7].

Primarily used as a project management and product development framework[8], Scrum describes a framework (*as shown in Figure 1*) for the Incremental Delivery of complex products. The Scrum framework is primarily team based, and defines associated roles, events, artefacts and rules. The origins of Scrum trace back to the mid-80s, but it was not a unified framework until 1995[9], when Jeff Sutherland and Ken Schwaber brought together the related experiences and research on Incremental product development and project management.

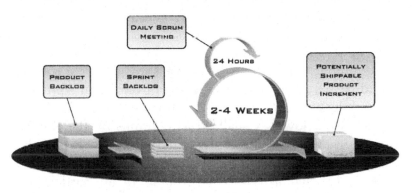

Figure 1: Scrum framework – Mountain Goat Software (CC-AT)

---

7 *Scrum Guide*, Schwaber and Sutherland (2011).

8 *Agile Software Development with Scrum*, Schwaber and Beedle, (2002).

9 *Business Object Design and Implementation*, Sutherland and Schwaber (1995).

Kanban

The original concepts of Kanban (カンバン) were developed in the 1940s and 50s by Taiichi Ohno[10] as part of the Toyota Production System, as a mechanism to control Just-In-Time (JIT) production and manufacturing processes. Kanban, which approximately translates as 'signboard', is described as a 'visual process management system that tells what to produce, when to produce it, and how much to produce'. The modern Kanban method, as formulated by David J Anderson in 2007[11], is an adaption of the original JIT approach, with an emphasis on staff welfare and continuous process improvement practices.

Just-In-Time: A production strategy that strives to improve a business return on investment by reducing waiting inventory and associated carrying costs.

At its simplest, each prioritised Task (or Card) on a Kanban Board passes through a visualisation of the Team's process, or workflow, as they happen. Each primary activity in the Team's workflow is visualised as columns on the Kanban Board, usually starting at Task definition, and finishing with delivery to the Customer. Of course, being Agile, these Cards and activities are visible to all participants, including the Customer. Figure 2 shows the actual Kanban Board used to track the writing of this book.

---

10 *Toyota Production System: Beyond Large-Scale Production*, Ohno (1988).

11 *Kanban: Successful Evolutionary Change for Your Technology Business*, Anderson (2010).

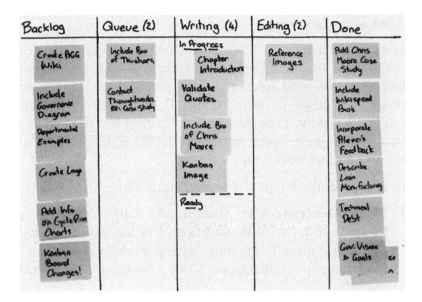

Figure 2: Kanban Board

Task: A discrete activity that forms a subset of a Requirement. Put another way, the delivery of each Requirement requires the delivery of one, or more, Tasks.

To identify, and control, bottlenecks and process limitations, each workflow state (or column) has a limit, called a WIP, or Work In Progress Limit, to the number of currently Active Tasks. This allows managers and Team Members to regularly monitor, and measure, the flow of work.

Lean Manufacturing

Lean Manufacturing, often called lean production, or just 'Lean', is a streamlined manufacturing and production technique, as well as a philosophy that aims to reduce production costs, by eliminating all 'wasteful' processes. Put another way, Lean focuses on 'getting the right things to the right place, at the right time, in the right quantity, to achieve perfect workflow'.

Lean defines three types of waste: Mura, Muri, and Muda.

1 **Mura (Unevenness):** Mura exists where there is a variation in production workflow, leading to unbalanced situations, most commonly where workflow steps are inconsistent, unbalanced, or without standard procedures.

2 **Muri (Overburden):** Muri exists where management expects unreasonable effort from personnel, material or equipment, most commonly resulting from unrealistic expectations and poor planning.

3 **Muda (Waste):** Muda is any step in the production workflow that does not add direct value to the Customer. The original seven wastes, as defined by the Toyota Production System (TPS), were Transport, Inventory, Motion (moving more than is required), Waiting, Overproduction, Over Processing (from poor design), and Defects (the effort involved in inspecting for, and fixing, defects). Additional and new wastes are not meeting customer demand, and are a waste of unused human talent. There is further differentiation between Type 1 (necessary waste, e.g. government regulations) and Type 2 (unnecessary waste).

Introduction

Based on the original Toyota Production System (*see section: Kanbans*), Lean Manufacturing was formally defined in 1988 by John Krafcik, and later expanded upon by James Womack, Daniel Jones and Daniel Roos[12].

Lean Manufacturing provides a set of techniques[13] to identify, and eliminate, waste which, in turn, improves quality, and reduces overall production time and cost. In addition, Lean Manufacturing also improves the 'flow' of production through the system. These techniques include:

- **Value stream mapping:** Analysing and planning the flow of materials and information that is required in the production process.

- **Five S:** This is an approach to quality and continuous improvement. The five Ss are: Sort (to clean and organise the work area), Set in Order (arrange the work area to ensure easy identification and accessibility), Shine (mess prevention and regular maintenance of the work area), Standardise (create a consistent approach for carrying out production processes), Sustain (maintain the previous four Ss through discipline and commitment).

- **Kanban:** *See section: Kanbans.*

- **Fail-proofing:** Prevent human errors before they occur.

- **Production levelling:** Ensure that each step in the production process delivers at a constant rate, so that subsequent steps can also deliver at a constant rate. No step in the production process should produce goods at

---

12 *The Machine That Changed the World*, Womack, Jones and Roos (1991).

13 *Lean Production Simplified*, Dennis (2007).

a faster rate than subsequent steps, or consume goods at a slower rate than preceding steps.

Finally, Lean Manufacturing emphasises Kaizen[14] (改善) or Continuous Improvement; the ongoing, incremental and regular technique of improving all processes, products and functions relating to production, resources, organisational management, and the supply chain.

 Kaizen: A philosophy, culture and technique of driving continuous improvement in work processes and business functions.

Many of the terms in Lean Manufacturing have been translated from the original Japanese. As such, they often lose the context, or secondary meanings, of the term. Where possible, this context is described throughout the book.

Feature Driven Development

Feature Driven Development (FDD) is a series of Agile processes to support the planning, design and building of large-scale projects[15]. Developed by Jeff De Luca in 1997[16], FDD defines five basic activities that break down complex systems and requirements into staged components suitable for Incremental development. These activities are:

---

14 *Kaizen (Ky'zen), The Key to Japan's Competitive Success,* Imai (1986).

15 *A Practical Guide to Feature-Driven Development,* Palmer and Felsing (2002).

16 *Java Modeling In Color With UML: Enterprise Components and Process,* De Luca, Coad and Lefebvre (1999).

1 **Develop overall model:** Define the context, and create a high-level scoping document.

2 **Build feature list:** Decompose the model into subject areas, and within each subject area, a set of features to be delivered (as with other Agile frameworks, the effort to deliver each feature should not exceed the length of a single Iteration).

3 **Plan by feature:** Prioritise, and assign, each feature to a development team.

4 **Design by feature:** Select, and design, the set of features to deliver in the current Iteration.

5 **Build by feature:** Build, test and review each feature.

Each activity is comprehensively discussed and peer-reviewed to ensure clarity and agreement between all stakeholders.

Test-Driven Development

Developed in 2003 by Kent Beck[17], Test-Driven Development (TDD) is primarily a software engineering process that forces programmers to write small, incremental verification tests prior to writing each function of the software. Each set of verification tests defines the outcome of a single feature or improvement. This 'test first' approach encourages simple design, concise development, and confidence in the product.

There are six steps to the TDD process:

1 Write new tests.

2 Run all tests, verifying that the new tests fail.

---

17 *Test-Driven Development by Example*, Beck (2003).

3 Write the software function.

4 Run all tests, verifying that the new tests pass. If the tests fail, or you discover any new issues, return to step three.

5 Refactor the code by improving the quality of work, without changing the functionality.

6 Repeat.

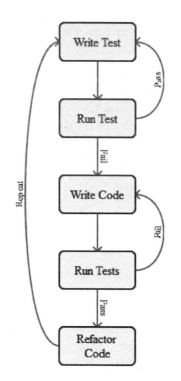

Figure 3: Test-Driven Development flowchart

TDD does not directly translate outside of a technical environment, where tests can be automated and strictly defined. However, you can apply the core concepts, and define the acceptance, quality control and quality assurance criteria prior to any work commencing, to the same benefit.

Quality Control: The act of identifying defects by testing, validating and verifying a completed product, or service, against the Customers' Requirements.

 Quality Assurance: The process of improving development and test processes, to increase overall quality and reduce defects.

 Defect: A shortcoming, imperfection, or lack in an otherwise completed Requirement.

Extreme Programming

Extreme Programming (XP) is an Agile software development framework created by Kent Beck and published in 1999[18]. Like all Agile frameworks, it advocates Incremental Delivery and responding to changing Customer Requirements. XP's focus is on the method and role of the Delivery Team, and defines four, basic activities within the software development process.

1 **Coding:** The act of building a working product to the specific Customer Requirements (code is also used as a communication and problem-solving tool; by attempting to code a solution, developers can discuss complex problems and demonstrate alternative solutions).

2 **Testing:** With strict emphasis on testing, especially automating testing, developers can ensure high-quality code, and the completeness of their work.

---

18 *Extreme Programming Explained: Embrace Change*, Beck (1999).

3 **Listening:** Getting the developers to communicate with the Customer ensures that both parties understand the Requirements, and effort, involved in delivery.

4 **Designing:** By emphasising planning and design, complex systems can be simplified, and unwanted dependencies reduced.

Common misconceptions

> 'On two occasions I have been asked, "Pray, Mr Babbage, if you put into the machine wrong figures, will the right answers come out?" [...] I am not able rightly to apprehend the kind of confusion of ideas that could provoke such a question.'

Charles Babbage, 1864

Being a generic term, Agile means different things to different people. Therefore, before we go much further, I should clarify some of the more common misconceptions surrounding Agile.

Agile is ad hoc, with no process control: First of all, Agile isn't a lack of process. Agile provides a range of formal processes, and methods, to inform work processes, customer engagement and management models. Conversely, Agile isn't about blindly following the prescribed 'agile' methods and processes. Agile is about using your common sense to apply processes, as determined by the current situation, and shaped by the Agile philosophy.

Agile is faster and/or cheaper: Agile isn't significantly faster, or cheaper, than alternative frameworks. Put another way, in most cases you can't get significantly more effort out of your Teams by moving to an Agile approach. While there is an overall efficiency gain when utilising Agile methods, well-managed Agile and non-Agile Teams will deliver products and services in approximately the same time and effort.

Agile teams do not plan their work or write documentation: Agile is not an excuse to avoid appropriate planning or writing documentation. It is an on-demand, or Just-In-Time, approach that encourages continuous planning and documentation, but only when needed for specific Customer Requirements. This allows Customers and Teams to determine if the planning, or document, adds value to the process or product. It creates an opportunity to emphasise valuable documents, and eliminate anything that isn't useful.

An Agile project never ends: While this may be true in some situations, the benefit of Agile is that work will continue while the Customer continues to gain business value, and that value is worth more than the cost of developing it. Most projects, in any industry, have a point of diminishing returns. This is the ideal time for an Agile project to end.

Agile only works for small organisations: Agile works for projects, teams and organisations of any size, not just small projects. That is not to say that it will work for *all* organisations, but size is rarely a factor. Large and complex projects and organisations are often excellent candidates for Agile transformation, where it is difficult, or impossible, to know all your Customer's Requirements in advance.

Without upfront planning, Agile is wasteful: This assumes that your Customer knows the detail of all of their

Requirements in advance. If this is true, then by all means, undertake comprehensive upfront planning. However, in reality this is rare, and usually leads to the greater 'waste' of having undertaken design and development work that was ultimately unnecessary. Agile Business Management encourages minimal upfront planning, ensuring everyone is working towards the same goal, and reduces the risk of miscommunication.

Finally, Agile is not **the solution to all your problems**. It is a change in approach and culture that comes with its own set of benefits and issues.

Governance and Agile Business Management

Q 'A leader is best when people barely know he exists, [...] when his work is done, his aim fulfilled, they will say: we did it ourselves.'

Laozi, ~6th Century BCE

Governance supports the organisation, by ensuring consistent management, cohesive policies, overall guidance, and decision-rights for a given area of responsibility. Though the structure, roles and policies may differ from traditional organisations, Agile Business Management uses these same governance mechanisms and controls.

Good management is about getting hundreds, if not thousands, or hundreds of thousands, of your employees all working in harmony towards a common goal. In most organisations, employees work on behalf of the shareholders, via the Board of Directors. All but the smallest of companies need strong governance processes to ensure consistent outcomes in-line with the expectations of the Board. Corporate governance defines these relationships, and provides the processes to ensure managers make appropriate business and financial decisions, managing staff and their Deliverables, and adequately controlling quality processes.

Deliverable: The product, or service, created by the Team (or Teams), to fulfil a specific Requirement. Each Deliverable generally only fulfils a single Requirement, so a large project may consist of many Deliverables.

There is no single model of good business management or corporate governance[19]. However, across the many approaches, including Agile Business Management, there are common themes, independent of industry, country or structure.

Corporate governance specifies the instruments to define, achieve, and measure your corporate objectives, in the interests of the company and its shareholders. Good corporate governance also puts in place appropriate monitoring controls, to ensure that the Board and executive bodies are actively pursuing these objectives.

Most organisations define governance through organisational structure, roles and responsibilities, and formal policies. Governance can also mean 'external governance'; strict controls and policies imposed on an organisation by external parties. These can include:

---

19 *OECD Principles of Corporate Governance*, Organisation for Economic Co-operation and Development (2004).

- Legislation; such as workplace relations, or occupational health and safety.

- Specific industry standards and frameworks; such as CMMI®, ISO9001, ISO20000, ISO38500 or the OECD Principles of Corporate Governance.

- Government and industry regulation; such as financial or tax regulation.

- Shareholder requirements and expectations.

Agile Business Management is nothing, if not adaptable. If compliance with a specific regulation conflicts with your Agile Business Management goals, adapt your goals and governance processes.

Agile Business Management also provides built-in verification points, to ensure governance compliance. These include:

- Escalation of decision approval to appropriate levels

- Transparency and oversight of decisions

- Reporting to external agencies

- Providing, and archiving of, documentation

- Formal audits of business practices.

All governance processes need to balance the needs of diverse stakeholders, including; shareholders, regulators, corporate functions, and internal Departments. For the interests of these stakeholders to be satisfied, there needs to be an alignment of corporate interests and objectives. Misalignment comes in many forms, including differing backgrounds and priorities, complex or overloaded governance controls, different management values and principles, or just the complexities of running a large multisite, or multinational, organisation.

Department: A specific group within your organisation, responsible for a specific business function, subject area, service or product. Human Resources, Finance and Accounting, and Sales and Marketing, are all examples of departments. Departments may also be known as Groups, Divisions, Organisation Units, or Business Areas.

All Agile Business Management processes aim to establish shared objectives and improve communication, but the most important feature is that they have built-in automatic alignment and re-alignment features. These include feedback-driven process adaption, empowered workers, self-organisation, collaboration and regular delivery.

At the end of your Agile Business Management transformation, you will have a set of processes that encourage broad collaboration across your business, including integration with corporate strategy and other core corporate governance mechanisms.

Successful Agile Business Management

'Beautiful objects are wrought by study through effort, but ugly things are reaped automatically without toil.'

Democritus, ~4th Century BCE

Becoming an Agile organisation is an incremental process. There is no single point you say to yourself, 'Yesterday we weren't Agile, but today we are. Success!' However, you can say, 'Today we are more Agile than yesterday!' Your journey to become an Agile organisation can be formal, through a transformation programme, or informal, through ad hoc changes addressing problem areas. Regardless of the mechanism, your Agile journey begins with a set of clear organisational goals. Ask yourself; what is your organisation trying to achieve by becoming Agile?

As every organisation will have different goals, so the process to become Agile will differ as well. In general, goals relate to improving adaptability in a changing marketplace, driving higher quality work, improved Customer and staff satisfaction, sustainable management processes, or reducing overheads.

To validate that you have achieved your organisational goals, you need to create a set of specific, success criteria that define measurable targets for your staff and stakeholders. Success criteria should be concise, realistic and directly measurable. It is also important to include both quantitative success measures, based on facts and figures, and qualitative success measures, based on feedback and opinion.

You can quantitatively measure the success of your Agile journey from your organisational maturity, in four key areas: Staff, Customer Engagement, Technology and Processes. For example:

1 Staff maturity measures
   o Staff are trained, and experienced, in Agile Business Management and associated frameworks (training measure).
   o Staff have an understanding of the underlying reasons for moving to Agile Business Management (communication measure).
   o Staff are directly empowered to engage with, and deliver to, the Customers (action measure).

o Staff are skilled in the supporting tool-sets (training measure).

o Staff are conversant in the work, quality control and release procedures (action measure).

2 Customer engagement maturity measures

o Customers are trained in their new responsibilities (training measure).

o Customers, or their representatives, are involved in the Team's daily activities (action measure).

o Customers actively define, and order, Requirements, at least once per Iteration (action measure).

o Customers have the authority to make decisions regarding the delivery of their Requirements (action measure).

3 Technology maturity measures

o There is a stable and well-documented supporting technology stack (*see section: Kanbans*) (action measure).

o The supporting technology has clearly defined ownership and service levels within the organisation (communication measure).

4 Process maturity measures

o Clearly defined business processes exist for all domains (action measure).

o Cross-domain interdependencies defined for all Departments (communication measure).

o Agreed service levels exist between all departments (communication measure).

o Each process has clear business ownership and delegations of authority identified (action measure).

Saying that staff attended training, is not sufficient to pass a training success measure. You must be able to demonstrate that staff can apply these new skills.

From a qualitative standpoint, there are only two main success measures:

1 Are our staff happy (action measure)?
2 Are our Customers happy (action measure)?

 To help differentiate them, you should phrase quantitative success measures as statements, and qualitative success measures as questions.

Not all organisations will succeed in becoming Agile. Organisation's with low morale, no staff or executive buy-in, high staff turnover, or a lack of trust between themselves and the Customer, need to address these issues at the beginning of any Agile transformation programme, and will introduce additional risk into the transformation.

Relationship to other management styles

'Human beings, who are almost unique in having the ability to learn from the experience of others, are also remarkable for their apparent disinclination to do so.'

Douglas Adams, 1990

Many of the concepts within Agile Business Management can happily co-exist with, and enhance, existing management and governance frameworks. This section looks at some common management frameworks and their interface points. The goal of this is to show that Agile Business Management does not exclude your existing management processes, frameworks or styles. You need to find the interactions between them, and create a management and governance framework that works for you and your organisation. The design of Agile Business Management is deliberately generic, so you can tailor the frameworks and concepts as appropriate to your organisation.

OECD Principles of Corporate Governance

The OECD Principles of Corporate Governance[20] is a set of common, corporate governance standards and guidelines for companies, investors, stock exchanges and related parties, in both OECD and non-OECD countries. There are six core principles. These relate to:

1 Ensuring the basis for an effective corporate governance framework.

2 The rights of shareholders and key ownership functions.

3 The equitable treatment of shareholders.

4 The role of stakeholders in corporate governance.

5 Disclosure and transparency.

6 The responsibilities of the board.

These principles complement the principles of the Agile manifesto, which guide Agile Business Management. Common to both, is an emphasis on transparency (*see*

---

20 *OECD Principles of Corporate Governance*, Organisation for Economic Co-operation and Development (2004).

Chapter 3: The Structure of an Agile Organisation) and accountability (*see Chapter 1: You, the Agile Manager*), at all levels across your organisation. The roles and responsibilities of the Board (*see section: The Board and executive governance bodies*) also extend to include greater participation and open communication.

Process control loops

Process control loops, such as Deming's Plan-Do-Study-Act (PDSA)[21], the related Plan-Do-Check-Act (PDCA), Six-Sigma's Define-Measure-Analyse-Improve-Control (DMAIC)[22], Test Driven Development's Red-Green-Refactor (RGR), and the military Observe-Orient-Decide-Act (OODA)[23] methods are cyclical processes to improve major decision making, through the rigorous testing of outcomes. Taking PDSA as an example, there are four key steps in the control loop; Plan, Do, Study and Act.

- **P:** Plan and set the objective upfront

- **D:** Do, or implement, the plan

- **S:** Study the results, and compare against the expected results

- **A:** Act on the results to improve the process

Agile Business Management iterates through a PDSA cycle for each Customer Requirement, and applies rigour to the upfront planning and quality processes. However, unlike

---

21 *The New Economics for Industry, Government, Education,* Deming (1993).

22 *JURAN Institute's Six Sigma Breakthrough and Beyond – Quality Performance Breakthrough Methods,* De Feo and Barnard (2005).

23 *The Essence of Winning and Losing,* Boyd, n.d.

many traditional PDSA processes which cycle through large blocks of work, this cycle repeats regularly and iteratively.

Another example is Test-Driven Development's (*see section: Quality control*) Red, Green, Refactor control loop, where Quality Control Tests are defined upfront, prior to your teams commencing any work. Once a Requirement is Done, the original tests run against the outcomes, to verify the overall completeness and accuracy. In this context;

- **Red:** Create the Quality Control Tests (which, if run, would obviously fail at this stage)

- **Green:** Do the minimum work to pass the Quality Control Tests (until the tests turn green)

- **Refactor:** Improve the quality of the work, to ease future enhancements and maintenance

You can also define the Red-Green-Refactor cycle as a PDCA control loop:

- **P:** Create the Quality Control Tests

- **D:** Do the work

- **C:** Validate the outcomes against the original tests

- **A:** Rework, or refactor, based on the results

 Quality Control Test: A formal procedure that identifies potential defects, by examining the specific output of a Deliverable.

Existing process control loops can also complement the continuous improvement processes (Kaizen) defined within the Agile Retrospectives chapter (*see Chapter 6: Reflection, Retrospectives and Kaizen*).

 Retrospective: A regular Team meeting to review, and reflect on, the management processes that support the day-to-day operation.

Deming's 14 points

Along with PDSA, Deming is also famous for his 14 points to managers for transforming business effectiveness[24]. These points aim to change the focus of management from growth through financial returns, to the more Agile approach of growth through investment, innovation and strong staff engagement.

1 Create constancy of purpose toward improvement of product and service, with the aim to become competitive, stay in business and to provide jobs.

2 Adopt the new philosophy. We are in a new economic age. Western management must awaken to the challenge, must learn their responsibilities, and take on leadership for change.

3 Cease dependence on inspection to achieve quality. Eliminate the need for inspection on a mass basis by building quality into the product in the first place.

4 End the practice of awarding business on the basis of a price tag. Instead, minimize total cost. Move towards a single supplier for any one item, on a long-term relationship of loyalty and trust.

---

24 *Out of the Crisis*, Deming, pp.23-24: Fourteen Points© Massachusetts Institute of Technology, by permission of MIT Press (1982).

5   Improve constantly and forever the system of production and service, to improve quality and productivity, and thus constantly decrease costs.

6   Institute training on the job.

7   Institute leadership. The aim of supervision should be to help people and machines and gadgets do a better job. Supervision of management is in need of overhaul, as well as supervision of production workers.

8   Drive out fear, so that everyone may work effectively for the company.

9   Break down barriers between departments. People in research, design, sales, and production must work as a team, in order to foresee problems of production and in use that may be encountered with the product or service.

10 Eliminate slogans, exhortations, and targets for the work force, asking for zero defects and new levels of productivity. Such exhortations only create adversarial relationships, as the bulk of the causes of low quality and low productivity belong to the system and thus lie beyond the power of the work force.

11 a. Eliminate work standards (quotas) on the factory floor. Substitute leadership. b. Eliminate management by objective. Eliminate management by numbers, numerical goals. Substitute leadership.

12 a. Remove barriers that rob the hourly worker of his right to pride of workmanship. The responsibility of supervisors must be changed from sheer numbers to quality. b. Remove barriers that rob people in management and in engineering of their right to pride of workmanship. This means, inter alia, abolishment of the annual or merit rating and of management by objective.

13 Institute a vigorous program of education and self-improvement.

14 Put everybody in the company to work to accomplish the transformation. The transformation is everybody's job.

The processes defined in Agile Business Management encapsulate most of these principles. For example, *Chapter 1: You, the Agile* Manager defines new responsibilities for Agile management. The Agile Retrospective process of review and reflect (*see Chapter 6: Reflection, Retrospectives and Kaizen*) creates a culture of continuous quality and process improvement. And the creation of effective, cross-functional and empowered Teams, that have the authority and accountability to deliver, is at the very heart of Agile Business Management (*see Chapter 3: The Structure of an Agile Organisation*).

Theory of Profound Knowledge

Q 'A system cannot understand itself. [The aim] is to provide an outside view, a lens, that I call a system of profound knowledge. It provides a map of theory by which to understand the organisations that we work in.'

W Edwards Deming

The Theory of Profound Knowledge[25] is the principle that an organisation is a complex system, made up of interdependent components, such as processes and people. The successful management of the interactions between its components, directly drives the success of the system.

---

25 *The New Economics for Industry, Government, Education*, Deming (1993).

Deming recommends that managers understand four things in order to manage the system effectively:

1 An understanding of the overall processes under their control.

2 Knowledge of variation, and how to measure it.

3 An understanding of the theory of knowledge itself.

4 Knowledge of psychology and human nature.

Understanding, and managing, the organisation as a whole, is a core requirement for any Agile manager. Without understanding the processes, and their expected variations, under your control, just-in-time planning is likely to have unexpected issues, with additional flow-on impacts. Similarly, without understanding psychology and human nature, it is difficult to manage cross-functional and self-organising Teams.

CMMI

Developed, and owned, by the Carnegie Mellon University[26], the Capability Maturity Model Integration[27] (CMMI), is not, in itself, a management framework. Rather, it is a set of goals and practices leading to corporate process improvement. However, CMMI does define a model for management best practices that an organisation must demonstrate, in order to show compliance. In all, CMMI assess organisations against 16 *core* process areas, as well as several context-specific process areas. Once appraised,

---

26 *Capability Maturity Model Integration*, Carnegie Mellon University; Software Engineering Institute, n.d.

27 CMMI® is registered in the US Patent and Trademark Office by Carnegie Mellon University.

organisations are given a maturity rating between one and five (Initial, Managed, Defined, Quantitatively Managed, Optimising), based on how well an organisation's processes compare to CMMI best practice.

The 16 'core' process areas are:

Project management

1 *Project monitoring and control:* A level 2 project management process to monitor, and manage, a project's performance against the plan.

2 *Project planning:* A level 2 project management process to establish, and maintain, plans that define project activities.

3 *Requirements management:* A level 2 project management process to control, and manage, project requirements through the lifecycle from planning to delivery.

4 *Integrated project management:* A level 3 project management process to manage a project and its stakeholders.

5 *Risk management:* A level 3 project management process used to identify, and mitigate, potential issues before they occur.

6 *Quantitative project management:* A level 4 project management process to verify that the project is meeting its performance and quality objectives, using quantitative measurements.

Agile Business Management emphasises strong project management governance, while remaining adaptable, and catering to changing Customer Requirements. Customer Requirements are tracked, managed, and delivered according to the Customer's priorities, which may change over the duration of the project (*see section: Requirements and the Requirements Backlog*). Standard Agile processes track, and regularly assess, risk (*see section: Risk management*). Finally, all work in Agile (whether project-based or not) is monitored, using comprehensive quantitative measurements. Continuous feedback is a core requirement to many Agile processes (*see section: Measuring progress*).

Support

7 *Configuration management:* A level 2 support process that manages the definition, and integrity, of deliverables across the lifecycle of development.

8 *Measurement and analysis:* A level 2 support process that manages the capability to collect, measure and analyse data on organisational processes.

9 *Process and product quality assurance:* A level 2 support process to evaluate processes, and deliverables, objectively.

10 *Decision analysis and resolution:* A level 3 support process to analyse possible management decisions, against formally established criteria.

11 *Causal analysis and resolution:* A level 5 support process that uses root cause analysis to identify the causes of selected outcomes, and uses that information to improve process performance.

Many of the recommended CMMI support processes form part of Agile Business Management. These include the use of the Requirements Backlog (*see section: Requirements and the Requirements Backlog*) as a configuration management technique, the quantitative measurement of progress, and the effectiveness of specific processes (*see section: Measuring progress*), as well as formal quality control mechanisms (*see section: Quality control*).

Process management

12 *Organisational process definition:* A level 3 process management process to define the organisational processes themselves, and the guidelines in their use.

13 *Organisational process focus:* A level 3 process management process to improve organisational processes, based on the incremental measurement of the success of existing processes.

14 *Organisational training:* A level 3 process management process to improve the skills, knowledge and capabilities of organisational staff.

15 *Organisational process performance:* A level 4 process management process to measure the performance of organisational processes quantitatively, to encourage continuous improvement.

16 *Organisational performance management:* A level 5 process management process to define business objectives, and proactively manage the organisation's performance, in order to meet them.

Process management and continuous process improvement, are important aspects of Agile Business Management. Using formal measurement (*see section: Measuring progress*), continuous feedback, and staff training (*see section: Managing Teams*), processes can be formally, and quantitatively, measured. The retrospective process (*see Chapter 6: Reflection, Retrospectives and Kaizen*) provides an integrated mechanism for process improvement to be discussed, planned and implemented.

In the latest version of CMMI (v1.3), effort has been made to map existing Agile techniques against CMMI process areas, to improve the accuracy of CMMI assessments in Agile organisations. In addition, there have been a number of case studies, and research papers, on the integration of Agile and CMMI, showing the benefits of a hybrid approach[28,29,30].

> '[Organisations] fail to distinguish that CMMI is fundamentally a model. Instead of working with CMMI as a model, they work with CMMI as a standard. A standard is an auditable, testable, compliable work with a narrow field of distinct, acceptable, and demonstrable outputs, with little variation from one implementation to the next...
>
> To reiterate from the model itself, "CMMI contains neither processes nor procedures;" the lists of typical work products, for example, are examples of process outputs.'[31]

This is not to suggest that Agile Business Management and CMMI work together seamlessly, or 'out of the box'. Organisations applying strict Agile Business Management would find it difficult to comply with some of the CMMI process areas at higher maturity levels. However, having said all that, you can tailor Agile Business Management to meet your organisation's CMMI requirements, while still following the values of Agile.

---

28 *CMMI® or Agile: Why Not Embrace Both!*, Glazer, Dalton, et al (2008).

29 *Extreme Programming from a CMM Perspective*, Paulk (2001).

30 *Love and Marriage: CMMI and Agile Need Each Other*, Glazer (2010).

31 *CMMI® or Agile: Why Not Embrace Both!*, Glazer, Dalton, et al (2008).

CHAPTER 1: YOU, THE AGILE MANAGER

'Knowing others is intelligence; knowing yourself is true wisdom.

Mastering others is strength; mastering yourself is true power.'

Laozi, ~6th Century BCE

Aim of this chapter: To make you think about your role as a manager. We investigate what makes a good manager, as well as examining your new, and changing, responsibilities under Agile Business Management. By the end, you should have the techniques you need to manage your staff, while empowering them to take direct responsibility and authority for their outcomes.

If you skipped the *Introduction*, Agile Business Management is a set of adaptive, lightweight, high productivity, and low waste business processes, designed to deliver regular outcomes for your Customers. As an Agile Manager, you need to understand, and embody, these concepts, and continuously develop, and encourage them, within your staff. Whilst it might be bad for the ego, you need to understand that you don't deliver anything, your Teams do.

Your primary job as an Agile Manager is to encourage and empower your Teams, therefore the first question becomes, 'How do you empower your Teams?' At a superficial level, it requires a simple, organisational change, to give each

Team Member sufficient personal responsibility, accountability *and* authority, to deliver the Customers' Requirements. Whilst that may be sufficient for some staff, getting others to *accept* that accountability and authority can be difficult, and requires an attitude change, as well as the organisational change.

> Remember Agile value #1: **We value individuals and interactions** over processes and tools.

In order to accept their new accountability and authority, your staff need the support of the organisation in three ways.

1 Firstly, they need to feel safe. Everyone makes mistakes, and one of the traditional roles of management is to buffer staff from these mistakes. In an empowered Team, where that buffer no longer exists, staff and management need to understand that while they must take every effort to avoid them, mistakes are inevitable, and, except in the most serious cases, acceptable. By putting in place self-correcting and transparent processes (*see Chapter 4: Work, the Agile Way*), Teams can proactively avoid mistakes, and learn from those that do occur.

2 Secondly, if you are expecting Teams to take authority, they must have all the information necessary to make appropriate decisions. Teams will generally already know the technical details, but, as a manager, you need to keep them aware of the context, the 'why' of the Requirements they are undertaking. By providing this context, your Teams will make more appropriate, strategic, and long-term decisions. This, in turn, will

empower them to be personally accountable for those decisions.

3 Finally, staff need to be able to make decisions, confident that management will uphold them. The simplest mechanism for this is to allow staff to make decisions without approval, within agreed cost, time and scope tolerances. For example, a Team Member may take any decision within 10% of the allowed budget, such as outsourcing part of the work.

The point of this management approach is to engage staff at their level of need and motivation. Though it has its share of criticism, Maslow's hierarchy of needs[1] is a useful model of human psychological needs. Figure 4 shows the basic hierarchy, from basic physiological needs at the bottom of the pyramid, to abstract self-actualisation at the top of the pyramid. As people fulfil the requirements of each category of need, they begin to be motivated by the next level. Traditional employment exists towards the bottom of the pyramid (safety), so to fully engage and motivate your staff, requires you to meet higher, and more abstract, needs. Agile Business Management focuses on engaging staff at the level of 'self-actualisation', by emphasising creativity, problem solving and personal empowerment.

---

1 *Motivation and Personality*, Maslow (1987).

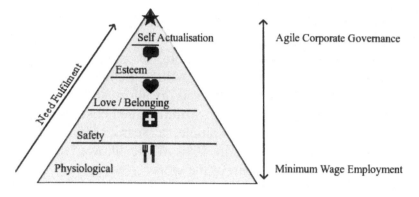

Figure 4: Maslow's hierarchy of needs

Remember Agile principle #5: Build projects [Teams] around motivated individuals. Give them the environment and support they need, and trust them to get the job done.

Consider for a moment, your management style. Dr W Edwards Deming[2] put forward two types of mistakes that you, as a manager, can make when dealing with 'variation' in process and outcomes. Interfering, or tampering, when everything is normal and within tolerance (common causes), which is indicative of micromanagement. Secondly, failing to intervene when a process is out of control (special causes), which is indicative of absenteeism. As an Agile Manager, or in fact any manager, you need to find the middle ground between these two extremes.

Micromanagers tend to be highly reactive to minor, expected, or manageable, issues without giving their Teams the authority to resolve them internally. If a process is under control, and within allowed tolerances, Team

---

2 *Out of the Crisis*, Deming (1982).

Members should have the authority to deliver, without management intervention. This assumes a robust monitoring and reporting process, to identify when management intervention becomes required.

This brings us to the other extreme, an absentee manager. A manager is 'absentee', even if they are physically in the office, if they do not monitor or engage with their Teams to ensure delivery. Without a manager to eliminate external, and sadly sometimes, internal impediments, it becomes nearly impossible to meet any schedules or budgets.

> Do not assume that a variation is due to special causes, when in fact it is due to common causes, or, more rarely, assume that a variation is due to common causes, when in fact it is due to special causes.

These are the attributes of a bad manager; but what attributes would make you a successful Agile Manager? While that could be an entire book in itself, I would condense them into 11 core attributes:

1 You have excellent problem-solving and decision-making skills, and can validate the pros and cons of a decision, while dealing with uncertainty and ambiguity.

Benefit: You take advantage of change, while reducing management overhead for your Teams.

2 You have excellent facilitation, communication and social skills, capable of presenting, negotiating, resolving, engaging and persuading. A quick wit and good sense of humour helps with this.

Benefit: You build relationships with Customers and colleagues, and reduce misunderstanding and conflict.

3 You are creative and innovative, and can develop, or recognise, new and unique responses to problems.

Benefit: You improve outcomes for your Customers, and reduce costs for your business. Creative managers also tend to attract talented staff.

4 You have strength of character when dealing with stress. You maintain self-control, and keep emotions out of professional interactions and decision making.

Benefit: You make appropriate decisions, and build a professional environment where your staff are comfortable around you.

5 You are aware of your strengths and weaknesses, and how they apply to your role as a manager. Staff will respond well to self-confidence, but not to a large ego.

Benefit: You can play to your strengths, and pro-actively improve your weaknesses. You can also avoid situations where others could exploit your weaknesses.

6 You are self-motivated, without needing constant supervision from others, and take accountability for organisational outcomes.

Benefit: You build trust with your superiors and colleagues.

7 You have the appropriate professional and technical knowledge needed to engage with your staff and Customers. You do not need to know how to do their job, but enough to understand their work.

Benefit: Your staff and Customers respect your opinion, which helps to resolve issues quickly.

8 You understand the value of delegation or 'getting things done through other people'. You trust your Team, and do not fear losing control.

Benefit: You will improve overall productivity, and promote personal development, by assigning work to the most appropriate people.

9 You manage your staff with honesty, fairness and integrity. You are willing to listen to, and seek input from, staff and are honest about performance, without being offensive or personal.

Benefit: Your staff feel trusted and empowered, leading to an environment where you can manage mistakes in an open and transparent manner.

10 You have flexible planning and time-management skills; visualising the short-, medium- and long-term requirements, while adapting to changing circumstances.

Benefit: You are in control of you, and your Team's work, leading to an overall reduction of stress, and an increase in productivity.

11 You are aware of the organisational strategy and your role within it.

Organisational benefit: Decisions factor in organisational goals, thus ensuring that all staff are working towards the same outcomes.

How then is an Agile Manager different from a traditional manager? In many ways, they are not very different; both have administrative control over finances, customer outcomes and staff management. The differences are in priorities, a shift to the middle ground between micromanagement and absenteeism; a hands off and consultative approach to your Team, and their duties.

Management responsibilities

Q 'Management of many is the same as management of few. It is a matter of organisation.'

Sun Tzu, ~6th Century BCE

At all levels, whether you are a team leader or CEO, as an Agile Manager you are responsible for facilitating day-to-day operation, managing risk, providing governance oversight, and directing the strategic outcomes of the organisation.

You will notice that I did not say you were responsible for the day-to-day operation, but rather you were responsible for *facilitating* the day-to-day operation. This distinction is important in Agile Business Management, as it is the responsibility of each individual Team Member to deliver on the day-to-day Requirements. I will explore this concept further throughout this book.

In the process of doing their job, Team Members will often identify business, technical, or personal issues, that they cannot resolve, and need to be escalated. Given the flat structure of an Agile organisation, it does not take much to escalate an issue to the CEO, so processes need to be in place to resolve them as early as possible. If, as a manager, you can resolve a business or technical issue immediately, you should do so, and not postpone it until a *convenient* time. Meetings and discussions to resolve complex issues should involve appropriate parties from across the organisation. However, it is important to invite only directly impacted Team Members, to reduce wasted time. Depending on the timeframe required to resolve the issue, Teams may move onto other Requirements, or put in place temporary workarounds, so they can continue to deliver to the Customer on a regular basis.

When your Team makes a decision, you still need to have the appropriate governance and oversight to validate that the decision was the 'right decision', in the context it was made. You need to be able to support the ongoing implications and outcomes of that decision, particularly where it impacts outside of your direct authority. Ultimately, you need to be able to trust your Teams, which may require appropriate guidance and coaching.

Interpersonal issues and conflict can arise within an Agile Team, just as easily as a non-Agile team. However, the impact of conflict is much greater, given the accountability and collaboration required for an Agile Team to work effectively. As a manager, you must identify, and resolve, these issues early, before they affect the Team's productivity. Options available to you when dealing with interpersonal issues may include:

- Talk with involved parties, to identify grievances and potential, mutually agreed solutions.

- Bring in a professional conflict resolution facilitator.

- Put conflicting parties on formal performance management, or manage the conflict through corporate HR processes.

- Conflicting parties can be split across Teams; though this usually only transfers the issue to someone else.

- Terminate the employment of anyone breaching company policy.

Similarly, you should curb any negativity, even light-hearted negativity, about Customers or other departments. Though it is easy to complain, this does not help Teams to work with each other, and can quickly get out of hand. You should still follow up on the underlying cause of the complaint to improve overall organisational communication and productivity.

Q You need to have a zero tolerance policy towards bullying and harassment, from both staff *and* other managers.

It's not enough to be a reactive manager; you need to be proactive in building strong Teams. Teams need to learn how to work with each other, but more importantly, how to communicate with each other. Allocate time for Team Members to appreciate each other's skills, as people work best when there is trust and confidence in each other's abilities.

As an Agile Manager, you need to be part of your Teams. Make sure Team Members are not afraid to come to you with problems, and talk regularly with them, not just when things are going badly. Find out how they think and what they need, and always follow up. Finally, you can motivate each Team by ensuring they understand how their current goals and actions tie into overall organisational objectives.

1: You, The Agile Manager

The Agile mindset

'So Mr Edison, how did it feel to fail 10,000 times?'

'Young man, I didn't fail, I found 9,999 ways that didn't work'

Thomas Edison, anecdotal (on his invention of the incandescent light)

One of the concepts I will drill into you throughout this book is that of the 'Agile mindset'. An organisation can be Agile as long as they *act* with the right mindset and values, regardless of specific management frameworks or processes. So the question becomes, 'What is the Agile mindset'? Whilst there is a lot of discussion on this topic, and unfortunately no single answer, the core Agile values provide a good starting point.

1 We value **individuals and interactions** over processes and tools.
2 We value **working software** over comprehensive documentation.
3 We value **customer collaboration** over contract negotiation.
4 We value **responding to change** over following a plan.

Ask yourself; what does the 'Agile mindset' mean to you? My definition of an Agile mindset, is one that embraces change, accepts failure, and focuses on staff welfare and Customer outcomes.

Embraces change

An Agile mindset accepts that change can, and will, occur and that change can be caused by both internal and external factors. Where possible, you leverage this change directly for your Customers' benefit. You understand that change may be outside your control, but quickly adapt to take advantage of it.

Accepts failure

Failure is a necessary step in the process of learning. In the Agile community, there is an expression: Fail often; fail early. An Agile mindset would look at failure as an opportunity where 'There is no failure, only feedback'. This doesn't mean you need to think that failure is good. You still want to produce high-quality outcomes for your Customers. However, you do see failure as an opportunity for learning. You encourage staff to come forward with any failures as early as possible, without fear of recrimination, to avoid compounding the problem. Most importantly, you do not think of your staff as 'failures' when they fail, and do not react emotionally to failure (yours or other peoples). Finally, you are accountable for failure.

Staff and Customer focused

If your mindset is staff welfare and Customer outcome focused, you recognise that business is a partnership that needs continuous attention and support. You want to learn from your Customers, and innovate with their current, and future, interests in mind. You acknowledge that when your Customer has a problem, not only is it also your problem until it is fixed, but your responsibility to ensure it never happens again. You work with your staff to build, measure, and reward Customer satisfaction activities, regardless of whether they followed process, or their job description.

Changing your mind

As amazing as the human brain is, at times of stress it often falls to irrational thinking, which breaks the Agile mindset. Irrational thoughts may seem truthful and realistic, but are actually exaggerated, irrational, or clouded by faulty perceptions. As an Agile Manager, it is especially important that you understand your own patterns of thinking, so you can identify thoughts that may affect your work, and the effectiveness of Agile Business Management.

 Examples of irrational thinking seen during Agile transformations include:

- 'Our Customer was unhappy with our progress on an Iteration, therefore they are unhappy with us!'

- 'Our Customer is happy with our progress so far, but I know it won't last.'

- 'Our first attempted implementation of Agile failed, therefore Agile does not work!'

Your staff will appreciate a manager who is in control, is honest and realistic. If you can be aware of your thoughts, you can identify and filter opinions not backed by evidence. This ultimately ensures stability and accuracy in you, and your Team's work.

CHAPTER 2: INTEGRATED CUSTOMER ENGAGEMENT

'You can't build a reputation on what you are going to do.'

Henry Ford, 1951

Aim of this chapter: To raise questions about your Customers: who are they, what their needs and goals are, and how can you work together? We will look at collaboration techniques to deliver their needs efficiently, with minimal waste, and to everyone's satisfaction. Moreover, we will examine the need to invest in building trust and communication, in order to improve outcomes for both parties.

To be Agile is to adapt when circumstances change, and nothing changes more than your Customers' needs. The second domain of Agile Business Management is the regular, and ongoing, fulfilment of Customer needs, through a collaborative and Incremental approach. You can achieve this close collaboration by integrating your Customer directly within the work process, granting them co-ownership, as well as co-responsibility, for delivery. Under this collaborative Agile approach, your Customer's responsibilities include defining, and ordering, the major Requirements, working with the Teams to ensure appropriate outcomes, and undertaking quality control, including final User Acceptance Testing.

Remember Agile value #3: We value **customer collaboration** over contract negotiation.

Your Customer needs to dedicate time to work with the Team. However, there is no 'right' amount of time; it is dependent on the complexity of the Requirements, how close the Requirement is to completion, and the Team's specific needs at that time. At a minimum, during each Iteration, or for each Requirement, the Customer must be available at the start (to help with planning), the end (to review and sign-off), and as required by the Team. Regularly scheduled weekly, or twice-weekly, timeboxed meetings, encourage a close, collaborative relationship between your Customer and your Team.

 Remember Agile principle #4: Business people and developers [Team Members] must work together daily.

 Timebox: A fixed period allocated to an activity or specific event.

 Iteration: A repeating timebox of fixed duration, allocated to the delivery of one or more Requirements from a larger piece of work.

There are some drawbacks to this model, including the imposition of additional time from your Customer. If they are not willing to engage with you in an Agile way, either through a lack of interest or availability, it will be difficult for you to maximise your ability to respond to change. Poor communication, lack of subject matter experts, and mismanaged expectations, are all symptoms of a poorly engaged, or inappropriate, Customer.

While some Customers have legitimate reasons, such as regulatory requirements, for wanting traditional engagements models, others reject the Agile engagement model because they don't understand the overall benefits. Training your Customers in their new role and responsibilities will significantly improve the take-up and effectiveness of Agile processes. If this still fails, there is significant benefit from applying the other Agile Business Management processes, while using traditional Customer engagement strategies.

Do not mistake consumers for Customers. Consumers purchase products from you. An Agile Customer, who may also be a consumer, has the responsibility, and authority, to direct the delivery of the products or services.

Consumer: An individual, or organisation, that purchases products or services from you, but does not have any authority, or responsibility, in the design, and development, of the product/service.

Customer engagement in an Agile model requires trust, which can be defined across five distinct levels.

1 **Team:** The highest level of trust where the Customer and organisation share the same goals and outcomes.
2 **Identification:** Where the Customer has a personal relationship with specific Teams or individuals.
3 **Knowledge:** Where the Customer bases their trust on personal knowledge and experience with the organisation.
4 **Contract:** Where the Customer uses legally binding contracts as the mechanism to trust the organisation.

5 **Reference:** Where third party references form the basis of trust.

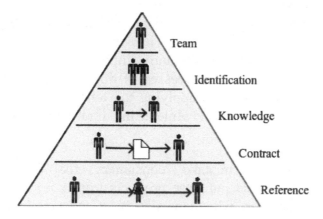

Figure 5: Customer trust levels

 Case study: Building trust with our Customers

A large retail body needed a specialist company to develop a marketing campaign for a new set of products. Our reputation as being one of the best companies in this field, along with several recommendations, led them to ask us to put forward a proposal (**Reference Trust**). We worked closely with the Customer to develop a proposal to meet their Requirements, which led to them engaging us to develop the marketing campaign (**Contract Trust**). By engaging with the Customer at all stages of the creation and delivery process, after several weeks our Teams delivered a marketing campaign to the satisfaction of the Customer (**Knowledge Trust**).

Several months later, this Customer needed another

marketing campaign, for a different product. Because of the relationship we had built with them, they approached us directly to discuss this new campaign (**Identification Trust**). Over the next two years, we successful delivered five new marketing campaigns. At this stage, we proposed, and the Customer agreed to, a partnership arrangement, whereby they retained us to provide ongoing marketing consulting and support across their organisation (**Team Trust**).

Customers who base their trust on references or contracts will initially find Agile difficult to accept. It is easier to be Agile with Customers who have personal experience, and personal trust, with your organisation.

What is a Customer?

 'A manufacturer is not through with his customer when a sale is completed. He has then only started with his customer.'

Henry Ford, 1922.

How you define your Customer is context specific, but is generally any person, group or organisation that requests, and usually funds, one or more Teams within your company, to deliver a set of Requirements. There are two types of Customers; external and internal.

Agile Business Management does not differentiate between Ultimate and Intermediate Customers.

Examples of Customers by context:

The Sales and Marketing manager (internal Customer) engages the graphic design Team (within Media and Communications) to re-brand their marketing material, in preparation for a new promotion.

An external client then engages the graphic design Team to re-brand their website. Though the Customers are different, in both instances the graphic design Team undertakes similar work, and closely engages with their current Customer to ensure successful delivery.

Directly connected to your organisation, an internal Customer can include senior management, employees, shareholders, external regulators, etc. The Customers for product oriented businesses are generally internal (e.g. a product or design manager), as the customers (little c) of these products are considered consumers, not Customers (big c). Exceptions are for organisations that are engaged directly to develop bespoke products, such as construction or software companies. Services delivered to internal Customers often relate to the operation of business, such as HR or IT support services.

External Customers are not directly related to your organisation, and usually engage your organisation to deliver specific outcomes. In general, service oriented businesses are engaged by external Customers, usually B2B, to deliver on specific Requirements.

 Your organisation will have many customers, but a Team's current 'Customer' is context specific, as defined by the Requirements.

 Examples of Customers by Team may include:

- *In a business intelligence team:* Your Customer could be the (internal) financial division requesting a financial report.

- *In a service delivery team:* Your Customer could be an (external) client generated through a sales Team.

- *In a retail team:* Your Customer could be an (internal) product manager. However, a Customer would not be someone walking into a shop front purchasing your product, this is a consumer. In general, there is an insufficient level of interaction to involve them in your business processes.

The Customer Representative

'The best executive is the one who has sense enough to pick good men to do what he wants done, and self-restraint enough to keep from meddling with them while they do it.'

Theodore Roosevelt, anecdotal

A Customer can delegate their responsibilities to an individual called the 'Customer Representative'. Common situations where this occurs are:

- The Customer is unavailable to fulfil their role.

- The Customer is a senior executive.
- There are multiple Customers.

The Customer Representative is an individual who has the authority to represent the Customer, and the Customer's Requirements, to your Team. From the Team's perspective, the Customer, and the Customer's Representative, are synonymous in both authority and responsibility.

 Customer Representative: An individual delegated with the authority to act on behalf of the Customer.

 Throughout this book, the term 'Customer' and 'Customer Representative' are interchangeable.

For those familiar with Scrum, the Customer Representative is equivalent to the Product Owner.

Requirements and the Requirements Backlog

'It is always wise to look ahead, but difficult to look further than you can see.'

Winston Churchill, ~1960

Now that you know who your Customer, or Customer Representative, is, it is time to start engaging with them on their Requirements. The first step, before the Customer creates any specific Requirements, is to define the vision, or goal, of the end state. This vision shouldn't be very complex, and can be as simple as a single sentence. For long projects or highly complex Requirements, you can create a simple, low detail, business case, to define the outcomes, non-functional requirements, and value of investing in the work. Because this is Agile, the vision will change as your Customer Requirements change, and it is important to keep the vision up to date, so all Team Members understand what they are working towards.

 Vision: A brief description of the expected end state after the Team completes all the Customer Requirements. This will change as the Customer Requirements change.

Example visions include:

- 'Recruit five new shop assistants for our new store.'

- 'The Corporate Branding Programme, through collaboration with our external partners, will strengthen our ability to promote, and sell, our range of products, by developing, and implementing, a coordinated brand across all our products, with associated shop fit-out and marketing collateral that is underpinned by comprehensive consumer research and staff training.'

- A simple five page business case for a new store system, with the following sections

1 Programme overview
   o   Objective
   o   Issue/opportunity to be addressed
   o   Strategic alignment
   o   Proposed solution
   o   In scope
   o   Out of scope

 o Constraints and assumptions

 o Dependencies

2 Outcomes and benefits

 o Tangible benefits

 o Financial benefits

 o Intangible benefits

3 Cost estimates

4 FTE estimates

5 Stakeholders

6 Programme milestones

7 Key risks

8 Options examined.

Once the vision is complete, the key artefact that your Customer is responsible for developing and maintaining, through the life of the work, is the Requirements Backlog. The Requirements Backlog is the ordered list of Requirements needed by the Customer. Given the collaborative nature of Agile, your Customer and Teams should create the Requirements Backlog together.

 Requirements Backlog: An ordered list of Requirements; maintained by the Customer, and estimated by the Team.

To minimise later rework, the initial Requirements Backlog should be created in low detail, and describe only the current and best-understood Requirements. The highest priority Requirements, those you will deliver next, are then expanded, with additional detail. Large Requirements that need more than a single Iteration to deliver, can be added to the Requirements Backlog, and later decomposed into smaller, self-contained Requirements. This ensures that the outcomes at the end of an Iteration are always usable, and deliver value to your Customer.

 Remember Agile value #4: We value **responding to change** over following a plan.

Each Requirement should meet the INVEST characteristics, as defined by Bill Wake[1].

- **Independent:** Each Requirement should be as self-contained as possible, with minimal dependencies on any other Requirement. This allows for easy reordering or removal, as Customer Requirement's change.

- **Negotiable:** The Customer can change a Requirement at any time, up to the point it enters the Iteration Backlog (*see Chapter 4: Work, the Agile Way*).

- **Valuable:** Each Requirement should deliver a tangible, and measurable, benefit to the Customer.

- **Estimatable:** The definition of each Requirement is such that the Team can estimate it.

- **Small:** The estimate, and delivery, of a Requirement, should be within a few days, or a single Iteration.

- **Testable:** Each Requirement should have appropriate quality control and quality assurance metrics, so the Customer can validate their Deliverables against the original Requirement.

The Requirements Backlog is the master document that defines the scope and high-level description of each Requirement. As work progresses, and your Customer's

---

1 *INVEST in Good Stories, and SMART Tasks*, Wake, n.d.

needs evolve, the Customer needs to keep the Requirements Backlog up to date. They can create, remove, change or reorder Requirements at will. Once all the Requirements are Done, and the Requirements Backlog is empty, the Backlog itself should remain, to cater for further changes as required by the Customer.

 Remember Agile principle #2: Welcome changing requirements, even late in development. Agile processes harness change for the customer's competitive advantage.

At a minimum, each Requirement within the Requirements Backlog should contain a User Story, in the following format.

As a [role]

I want a [goal/desire]

So that [benefit]

The [role] is the expected end-user of the Requirement, who is usually different from the Customer. The [goal/desire] of each User Story describes what should be delivered, and the [benefit] provides the context, or the Why.

User Story example – HR Team:

As a Team leader

I want someone with good technical writing skills

So that we can develop new tenders

User Story example – Sales Team:

As a sales consultant

I want new marketing material designed and printed

So that we can promote our new range of products

User Story example – Production/Operations:

As a bookstore retail chain

I want 1,000 copies of *Directing the Agile Organisation*

So that we can sell them to our customers

User Story example – Production/Operations:

As a bookstore retail chain

I want in-store promotional material for *Directing the Agile Organisation*

So that we can promote and market to our customers

In addition to the User Story, each high priority Requirement within the Requirements Backlog should contain the following information:

- **Order:** How soon should the Team deliver this Requirement? Risk, value and necessity to the Customer all drive the order.

- **Dependencies:** Are there any other Requirements that the Team need to deliver first?

- **Additional stakeholders:** Does the Team need to engage anyone else during the planning or development phases?

- **Quality control requirements:** What are the quality control steps to verify that the Requirement is Done?

- **Effort estimation:** What is the Estimate of the effort to develop the Requirement (*see section: Effort estimation*)? This is the only part of the Requirements Backlog developed by the Team, not the Customer.

Requirements should not require additional information, until they are at the top of the Backlog, and the Team is ready to work on them. If a Requirement is highly complex, and you feel it needs more information, consider splitting it into multiple, smaller Requirements. In addition, only the Team should define specific technical and implementation criteria, and only in the planning phase of delivery (*see section: Phases of delivery*).

To be successful, the Customer must take ownership of the Requirements Backlog, both its creation and ongoing maintenance.

If multiple Teams are working together towards the same outcome, for the same Customer, the Customer should only create, and maintain, one Requirements Backlog. You can dynamically group Requirements using whatever mechanism you need, such as related Requirements, skills, or Deliverables for each Team.

On a regular basis, or between each Iteration, your Customer must keep the Requirements Backlog up to date with their latest Requirements. This ensures that your Teams can meet the Customer's current needs, and that the next Requirement to be delivered is the most appropriate and useful. As they are Done, or deemed unnecessary, each Requirement should be removed from the Requirements Backlog, to ensure clarity, and reduce the risk of confusion.

By building the Requirements Backlog, Teams will:

- Reduce uncertainty within the Team when designing Tasks, which in turn reduces the risk to the Customer.

- Promote regular communication between the Customer and Team, which can also speed up decision making.

- Ensure that the Requirements integrate with current short-term and long-term goals.

- Identify required Team Members, which in turn will improve overall financial planning across the lifecycle of the Customer's Requirements.

- Ensure that the Team has a comprehensive understanding of the Customer's Requirements, without getting into too much detail.

 Example Requirements Backlog process:

Iteration #1: Planning

An HR Department needs to develop a new set of OH&S standards for one of their Customers, the OH&S committee. The Customer defines four Requirements within the Requirements Backlog.

1. *As an* office worker; *I need* to understand my rights and responsibilities when using ICT equipment; *In order* to comply with OH&S requirements.

2. *As a* manual labourer; *I need* to understand my rights and responsibilities when on a client site; *In order* to comply with OH&S requirements.

3. *As an* executive; *I need* to understand my rights and responsibilities when travelling; *In order* to comply with OH&S requirements.

4. *As an* employee; *I need* to understand my rights

and responsibilities regarding bullying; *In order* to comply with OH&S requirements.

Iteration #1: Estimation

The Team reviews, and estimates, this Requirements Backlog, prior to starting, so that everyone involved understands the effort involved, and the expected outcomes.

1. ICT use policies: Four days

2. Manual labour policies: Five days

3. Travel policies: Two days

4. Bullying policies: One day

Iteration #2: Planning

During the development of the first Requirement, the Customer updates, and reorders, the Requirements Backlog, and includes a new Requirement. This takes into account their current priorities, based on specific events happening in the company. Once again, the Team reviews, clarifies and re-estimates the new Requirements Backlog, before beginning work on the current top Requirement.

1. ICT use policies (Done)

4. Bullying policies: One day

2. Manual labour policies: Five days

5. Client site policies: One day

3. Travel policies: Two days

For Incremental Delivery, at the beginning of each Iteration, your Team groups the top Requirements from the Requirements Backlog into a new, high-detail, Iteration Backlog. Your Team then decomposes this Iteration Backlog into individual Tasks, and roughly estimates them, to ensure that delivery can occur within the Iteration timeframe. *You can find more information on the Iteration Backlog in Chapter 4: Work, the Agile Way.*

 Iteration Backlog: An ordered list of Tasks to be delivered during an Iteration.

CHAPTER 3: THE STRUCTURE OF AN AGILE ORGANISATION

Q 'Make everything as simple as possible, but not simpler.'

Albert Einstein (paraphrased), 1933

Aim of this chapter: To provide the organisational context in which Agile, and Agile Business Management, operates. We will look at the lean management structures that provide oversight, set goals and manage risk, whilst remaining flexible and adaptable. This chapter will also describe many of the specific management techniques needed to manage different types of Teams, Departments, and companies, in an Agile way.

The third domain of Agile Business Management is an organisational structure that promotes increased communication, trust and empowerment of your Teams. The ideal Agile Business Management structure has the minimum layers of management between the CEO, or equivalent, and junior Team Members, whilst still remaining efficient and functional. By creating self-organising and cross-functional Teams made up of individuals empowered with personal authority and accountability, a single, mid-level manager should be capable of supporting between 10-20 Teams. Each cross-functional Agile Team is typically between 5-9 full-time staff, where the whole Team works towards a single, specific outcome.

Cross-Functional: Where individuals with different, and complementary, skills, work together as a Team.

 Self-Organising: The responsibility of the Team to create a functional, internal Team structure, by replacing, and reorganising, Team Members as needed.

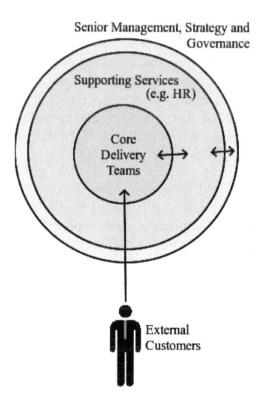

Figure 6: Simple Agile organisation structure

As shown in Figure 6, the heart of your Agile organisation is the many small, cross-functional, empowered, and in some cases, self-organising Teams. Each Team should contain all the key skills required to deliver on their Customers' Requirements. Benefits to this integration include faster delivery times, rapid response to new issues, and improved information sharing across the organisation. However, to realise these benefits requires that all Team Members are committed to the outcome, and adaptable in their role. This is different to the traditional hierarchical or matrix management structures, where one Team would start the process, and at pre-determined stages, request input from, or handover to, another Team. By passing work between silos, strict matrix organisational structures lack consistent ownership of work, cause poor communication between departments, and increase delays in the overall process.

You can expect your organisation to perform better under Agile Business Management, but only if everyone is pointing in the same direction.

 Example Cross-Functional Team:

A Team responsible for developing a proposal and quote for a new Government client, could include sales people, marketers, graphic designers, solicitors, technical writers, pre-sales technical experts, etc.

While the design of Agile Business Management is adaptable, to almost any organisation, to take advantage of the benefits, your organisational structure must be conducive to good communication and staff engagement.

Individual departments within an Agile organisation should contain all the required skills to deliver their Customers' (the department's Customers, not the organisation's Customers) Requirements. When your Teams identify that additional skills are required to deliver a new Requirement, they should have the authority to recruit, or transfer, staff with those skills into their Team. Agile organisations can utilise informal 'Centres of Excellence', or 'Competency Centres', as a mechanism to ensure that specific skills are managed and developed consistently, across the organisation. However, an individual needs to be able to utilise their judgement and common sense where appropriate. Common Centres of Excellence include; project management, business intelligence, quality assurance, communications and risk management.

 Create Centres of Excellence around skills that belong to a Team, rather than separate departments.

By consolidating the Customer Requirements into a specialised Requirements Backlog (*see section: Requirements and the Requirements Backlog*), new Teams can be dynamically established outside of traditional reporting hierarchies and departments. This is most useful to deliver project-based outcomes, or to develop prototype products for business research and development. After delivering their Requirements, you can either convert temporary Teams into a new department, or transfer them into an existing one.

 Remember Agile principle #11: The best architectures, requirements and designs, emerge from self-organising Teams.

The skills that make up a Team should be complementary, and specified by the Requirements of the Customer. New and existing Team Members take on various roles within the Team, based on their expertise, and taking into account the following five factors:

1 Individual Team Members will have specialisations and preferences, and whilst they should be able to take on different roles, they may not be as productive.

2 Team Members should be able to take on multiple roles, though they will not be able to take on ALL roles. You will need a good coverage of skills to ensure role coverage.

3 There is a productivity penalty for context switching; you want Team Members to focus on a specific role, and switch only as required.

4 Staff who can take on multiple roles, tend to be more creative in their work.

5 The Customer's Requirements drive the structure of the Team, and often require multiple Team Members in the same role to meet them.

 Example Cross-Functional Team:

A Team responsible for developing a proposal and quote for a new Government client may change during different Iterations of work.

Iteration 1	
As a procurement manager, *I want* a tender response that clearly defines the proposed solution.	Pre Sales Technical Writer Business Analyst

As a procurement manager, *I want* to see detailed costs for the proposed solution.	Finance
Iteration 2 *As a* procurement manager, *I want* the tender response to be attractive and easy to read.	Pre Sales Technical Writer Graphic Designer
...	...

By splitting Requirements into small and manageable parts, suitable for Continuous or Incremental Delivery, Teams can be restructured with different roles regularly, and as required. To ensure the correct distribution of roles and skills, your Teams need to plan each Iteration out in reasonable detail. Each Team should be responsible for planning the Iteration; including replacing Team Members, to ensure the correct combination of skills.

 Incremental Delivery: Planning and delivering related Requirements in short, fixed-time blocks.

 Continuous Delivery: Planning and delivering related, or unrelated, Requirements as they are identified and prioritised.

Reducing delays and bottlenecks is one of the key benefits to cross-functional and self-organising Teams. By individuals changing their primary role on-demand, the Team can deliver high-priority Requirements consistently, without waiting on external dependencies. By visualising the flow of work through each role, the Team can quickly identify bottlenecks, allowing them to self-correct, without requiring management decisions.

The next chapter covers the delivery and visualisation of Requirements in more detail.

Trust and authority are important factors in developing empowered Teams; this can be encouraged by ensuring that your Teams have direct ownership, and control, of their work, within the bounds set by the Customers' Requirements. To support the Team's ownership of their work, and prevent undue interference, Scrum introduced the concept of differentiating between Committed and Involved Parties.

The Team makes up the Committed Parties, those who are actively working towards delivering Requirements for the Customer, and are accountable for its outcome. Managers, Customers, Customer Representatives and other Stakeholders, are Involved Parties, those who have an interest in the outcome, and are consulted and kept informed of status, but are not responsible for day-to-day delivery. A successful outcome needs both Committed and Involved Parties; however, a successful Team must be sufficiently empowered, in return for taking accountability for delivery.

As with everything, cross-functional Teams are not without their risks. Understaffed Teams may not be able to deliver all the Requirements that the Customer needs. A Team may be lacking individuals with needed, specialised skills, or individuals may be unable to dedicate the time required to the Team, through either unplanned leave, or other corporate (non-Customer) requirements. By being aware of these, and related risks, you can put in place simple resource mitigation strategies. For example, allowing the Team to estimate, and plan, each Iteration themselves, delaying Requirements until a Team Member with a specific skill-set is available, clearly communicating with the Customer to set their expectations upfront, and putting in place good staff redundancy measures.

A possible mitigation strategy for some of these risks is to ensure that your organisation has a central skill register that all Team Members are responsible for keeping up to date. Noting, of course, that staffing is a highly complex issue, and has long-term impacts on Teams if poorly managed. The skill register should list the professional processes, techniques and technologies that Team Members are experienced in, their level of capability, and any related information (such as education or qualifications). This register should be centrally located and visible to all staff, to help Team Members self-organise, by identifying who, in your organisation, has the skills needed to deliver on their Customer's Requirements.

Estimate: The process of calculating the effort required to deliver a Requirement.

When recruiting for an Agile organisation, you need to place greater emphasis on people and communication skills. You are looking for staff that fit the Team culture, can accept accountability, do not require micromanagement, are multi-skilled, and can take on additional responsibilities as required. Where possible, you should never recruit new staff only to fill an immediate need. New staff should be engaged strategically, and time taken to integrate them into your organisational culture.

Your Agile HR Department should be working very closely with the Teams, their Customer, to ensure Requirements are being met. This engagement model means that each Team shares the authority for hiring candidates, and, as such, is ultimately accountable for that decision, and for hiring suitable candidates, with suitable skills, for their Team.

So far, I have mostly talked about the delegation of authority to empowered Teams; what then, is the role of management in an Agile Organisation? Each department, whether it supports internal or external Customers, needs management at an appropriate level. To continue the example from earlier, a HR Department may have two Teams, and multiple internal Customers, but still requires a single manager who is responsible for staff performance management, initial Customer and stakeholder engagement, and financial management and delegation. Ultimately, it is you, the Agile Manager, who is responsible for empowering, inspiring and leading their Teams (*see Chapter 1: You, the Agile Manager*).

Case study: IT Branch, City of Edmonton - Building an Agile organisation!

IT Branch, City of Edmonton: The IT Branch is responsible for managing, and maintaining, the IT investment across the City of Edmonton. Consisting of 340 people, five sections, and almost $60m in operating budget, the branch works with business units to help them translate business needs into technology solutions. Operating as a shared service, *their primary Customers are the internal business units that make up the City functions, such as fire, waste management and public transit.*

In 2008, the IT Branch received feedback from City staff and business leaders that they were not meeting service delivery expectations. To address these issues, and the related underlying causes, an enhanced, and sustainable, service delivery model was created. This model of service delivery, leadership and engagement was built around the following principles; listen, support, encourage and, most of all, deliver.

This new service delivery model was adopted by mid-2009, after significant engagement with all staff. To bring about the cultural changes needed for this new model, the IT Branch has spent the past four years undertaking business transformation, establishing structural change, educating staff, and implementing new processes.

The problems:

The two major problems that originally catalysed the transformation of the IT Branch were identified in the 2008 annual Customer survey and biennial employee survey.

1 Customers' needs were not being met.

2 The staff environment was fostering low morale.

These problems became even more apparent as people came to understand that the current approach to managing IT in local government was no longer working. That is, traditional approaches to building permanent systems no longer aligned with how things were functioning in reality. Ultimately, with the City demanding so much of the branch, there was no other option but to attempt an Agile and flexible solution.

The causes:

Over time, the City (which is now 107 years old) had become a very hierarchical, command and control organisation. This fostered an environment in which people did not feel encouraged to take responsibility for their actions, and was not suitable to meet the new challenges, and rapid evolution, in IT.

In addition, staff had much greater understanding, and expectation of technology than in the previous five or 10 years. As a result, the IT branch was constantly struggling to keep up with changing demands.

These problems, and their causes, are not unique to Edmonton. They are common across local government, and certainly exist in many other organisations.

The solution:

Over the last few years, there has been a huge reset in terms of people's expectations of leaders. People started to ask; 'How did leaders let it come to this?'. This led to a shift in thinking within the City, towards a new leadership model that encourages co-creation, engages staff, and leverages people's intrinsic motivations.

The solution was to move away from the concept of

a delivery manager (such as a client solution manager, or an infrastructure services manager), as these types of managers were often much better as technical experts, than as effective people managers. Structurally, the IT Branch went from seven directors to five, and from 31 managers, 11 of which managed no people (Figure 7), down to 20 technical managers and six coaches (Figure 8). A key part of the new structure involved taking a group of IT professionals, who could also be people managers, and converting them into coaches, responsible for engaging with staff and driving the cultural change.

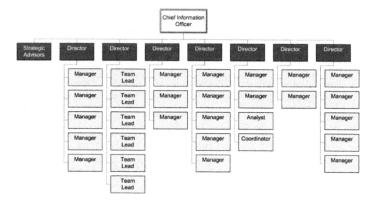

Figure 7: Pre-transformation organisation chart

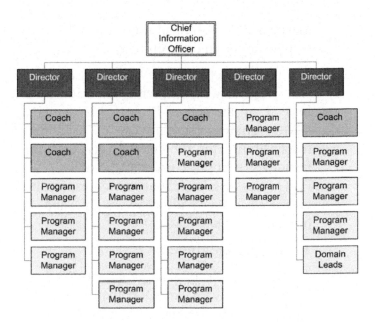

Figure 8: Current organisation chart

In parallel to the structural changes, the branch created a resource management office (RMO) to streamline the management of staff assignments. Operationally, everyone reports to the RMO, and is assigned to work based on their knowledge, skill, ability and availability. This is a very complex and difficult function, and the branch is still working to improve it. Finally, the creation of the RMO means that staff understand that the person they are working with today, might be reassigned to another project with a higher priority.

From a cultural perspective, it was important for the branch to keep using the word ownership. Historically, there hadn't been the concept of personal ownership; that outcomes weren't just the manager's responsibility, but everyone's responsibility, in different ways.

The final aspect to the new model was to change the way projects were implemented within the branch. Instead of an active Project Management Office (PMO) guiding the delivery of each project, the responsibility for project delivery, and the project resources, was put back into the delivery units. The PMO was retained, but their responsibility was refocused on providing oversight, and managing processes and standards.

The implementation:

As an approach to sustainable service delivery, the IT leadership team came together in March 2009 and proposed, what was then, the Agile Service Delivery (ASD) model. However, the response to the initial presentation of the ASD model to the IT Branch was almost universally underwhelming. People didn't respond to it, and the consensus was that it would be like all the other 're-orgs', lots of talk, but nothing would change.

This led to the realisation that, to the staff, it looked like the leadership team had gone into a room, cooked up a solution, and presented it to the branch as a 'fait accompli'.

In April 2009, it was decided that a new approach was needed. This resulted in a series of 30 town hall meetings, each with 10, randomly selected staff attending. The goal of these town hall meetings was to give staff an opportunity to talk about the current state, and their vision of the future.

In planning for these meetings, it was decided that what was discussed at each meeting would be posted for ALL to see. That was the first step to being transparent. At the beginning of each meeting, the two goals for the transformation were articulated to the staff, in order to provide context. These were:

1 To create fulfilment in their work.
2 To provide them with the freedom to do what they knew needed to be done.

In order to remain Agile and flexible, the original plan for an ASD model was put aside at the beginning of the town hall process. By the conclusion of the town hall meetings, the branch had adopted a model similar to ASD, but developed through co-creation with an engaged workforce. The major difference between the original ASD and the current model, was to move responsibility for project delivery from the PMO to operations staff, in order to retain, and share, experience.

At the conclusion of the town hall process, the entire branch met, to draw together all of the discussions, and chart a way forward. It was at this point that the leadership team sat down with HR, the unions, and other resources, to discuss the implications of the model. Using value management as a framework, the leadership team was then able to map from the values, and the '10 Ways of Being'[1], to the business model. From that, developed the mission and vision statement that was circulated to the whole branch for

---

1 *Transforming the City of Edmonton IT Branch*, Male (2009).

discussion.

In mid-2009, a project manager was engaged to formally manage the process of restructuring the branch, one level at a time. The project manager was responsible for the practical aspects of the transformation, such as the plans, rewriting the manager's job descriptions, creating the coach positions, moving people around, etc.

The branch restructure also emphasised the need for good governance from the IT leadership group. To ensure that all the directors were on the same page, and common issues were discussed, a regular leadership forum was established.

It wasn't until early 2011 that the project manager was assigned off the transformation. The change had reached a self-supporting stage, where it had become everybody's responsibility, not just the project manager, or the leadership team.

The challenges:

Most of the challenges faced during the early stages of the transformation, related to people's ability to cope with the change, and continue to operate in the new IT Branch.

The continuous change experienced within the branch transformation, led to a sense of instability, or insecurity, for staff. This was further compounded by the anxiety caused by unsubstantiated rumours and general speculation. Communication, and the overall communication strategy, became an integral part of the branch's ability to be Agile. Changing people's view from 'Oh, that didn't work, so we're trying something else now' to 'This is another aspect of our journey'. It would be incorrect to assume the branch has been 100% successful, but creating, and maintaining, a relationship of trust with staff, has built confidence in the transformation, and with the leadership team.

In addition to managing challenges at a group level, there was also the challenge of managing individuals. Many people had individual issues and concerns that blocked their ability to be successful. This is where the coaches became involved. The coaches were responsible for working closely with people, and addressing their individual concerns. Of course, this had to be balanced with the risk of spending all your time with the high needs people, and losing sight of the mission.

A good example of this is that people, in general, don't do a good job of holding other people, or themselves, to account. In the past, the hierarchy was the mechanism that held people to account. However, when the transformation moved away from that model, it became each staff member's personal responsibility to follow up, or recommit.

At the far end of the spectrum were those staff who did not engage. Those that said, 'I don't come to work for fulfilment, I come to work for the pay cheque'. This meant that the process of hiring people became very important. New recruitment priorities have been put in place to ensure that new staff don't just fit with the culture, but are going to help the branch move forward with the culture.

Finally, there have also been structural challenges

within the transformation. The roles and responsibilities of the RMO have been widely accepted, and it is understood that without it, the branch doesn't have the flexibility to move people to where they are needed. However, in many cases, a manager will still ask for a specific person, rather than whomever the RMO sends. For this to be properly resolved, an ongoing, and involved, cultural shift is required.

The outcomes:

As of early 2013, the IT Branch transformation has been in progress for over four years. Though worthwhile, the transformation has not been an easy process. It took several years for the directors and managers to get on board with the changes. Overall, the branch has reached a state where those who don't understand, and don't engage, are the odd ones out, responding in a different way to most of the others. This is true of both leaders and staff.

The best evidence for the success of this transformation is shown in the upwards trend, in terms of satisfaction, engagement and understanding, in the 2012 customer and employee surveys.

Over the last few years, in addition to the branch transformation, the entire City has adopted new, co-created, leadership principles. This new corporate approach aligns closely with, and validates, the approach taken by the IT Branch, to the point that the language is similar.

While this transformation has been a success, there

is still work to do in some areas. People ask 'When is the transformation going to be over?', and our answer is, 'Once started, it never ends'.

- Chris Moore, CIO, City of Edmonton

Internal departments

> 'A new type of thinking is essential if mankind is to survive and move toward higher levels.'

Albert Einstein, 1946

As an Agile Manager, you are responsible for one, or more, business functions or departments. Each department typically divides the organisation into functional areas, each with different outcomes, Customers and ways of working.

Human Resources

Human Resources (HR) is responsible for staff recruitment, salary management, and implementing management policies within an organisation.

- **Typical products:** HR policy documents, position descriptions, and job advertisements.
- **Typical processes:** Managing applications, verifying claims, personality tests (e.g. Belbin or Myers Briggs), industrial relations negotiations, salaries, separation procedures (both voluntary and involuntary), and performance management.
- **Optional processes:** Occupational health and safety, career counselling, and staff training.

- **Frameworks and guidelines:** Equity and Diversity legislation.
- **Typical Customer:** Internal departments.
- **Stakeholders:** Finance and Accounting (budget), Media and Communications (external advertisements).
- **Work style:** Ad hoc, suitable for Continuous Delivery.

The responsibilities of HR do not change dramatically under Agile Business Management, though there may be significant cultural changes. Changes are primarily to workflow, transparency and Customer interaction.

ICT Support and administration

ICT Support is responsible for the day-to-day administration of IT assets, including infrastructure (desktops, telephony, servers, network), and software (applications, the Internet/intranet, operation systems). Large organisations will generally have tiered support, and may even outsource the first tier (help desk).

- **Typical products:** ICT infrastructure, standard operating environment.
- **Typical processes:** Help desk support, system upgrades, preventative maintenance, system (e.g. desktop, telephony, etc.) provision, testing/installing new products.
- **Optional processes:** CT project management.
- **Frameworks and guidelines:** Product administration guidelines, ISO20000.
- **Typical Customer:** Individual staff members (via help desk), internal departments.

- **Stakeholders:** Privacy and security (policy and audit), Finance and Accounting (budget and procurement).

- **Work style:** Mostly ad hoc, suitable for Continuous Delivery. Some project based (e.g. system upgrades), suitable for planned Incremental Delivery.

The role of IT Support and Administration does not change dramatically under Agile Business Management. Like HR, changes are primarily to workflow, transparency and Customer interaction. Outsourced help desk functions can continue to be outsourced, but you will get improved interaction by removing, or making, the first tier transparent, and ensuring that support Teams are physically located in the same building as their Customers.

Sales and Marketing

Sales and Marketing Teams interface between consumers (or Customers) and the Delivery Teams. They are responsible for the promotion, pricing, market research, lead generation, and sale of your products and services. Effective Sales and Marketing Teams will interact closely with your Customers, through shop fronts, online websites, social media, or professional networks. Sales and Marketing also work closely with the Delivery Teams, to ensure that the outcomes meet Customer needs or expectations.

- **Typical products:** High-level product requirements, packaging.

- **Typical processes:** Lead generation, market research, setting prices, promotion, professional networking, presentations (e.g. conferences and trade shows), sales (online, shop front, or B2B), distribution.

- **Optional processes:** Advertising campaigns, social media, Customer service.

- **Frameworks and guidelines:** Relevant legislation.

- **Typical Customer:** The organisation (represented by the senior executive). Depending on your organisation, the Delivery Teams can be a Customer, but the converse is also possible, where the Marketing Manager is the Customer of the Delivery Teams.

- **Stakeholders:** Media and Communications (branding and advertising), Finance and Accounting (budget and cashflow).

- **Work style:** Ad hoc. Suitable for Continuous Delivery.

Sales and Marketing often work in an Agile way already, so under Agile Business Management their role may not change significantly. For B2B products, sales staff are still responsible for lead generation, but handover to the Delivery Teams is much earlier. Remember, Delivery Teams have the responsibility for working directly with the Customers. For B2C products, the marketing manager may become the Delivery Team's Customer, with the additional responsibilities that entails. There is minimal change to consumer sales Teams, e.g. shop front staff.

Finance and Accounting

Finance and Accounting is responsible for the management of all the financial and monetary aspects of the business.

- **Typical products:** Annual budget, tax returns, payroll.

- **Typical processes:** Cashflow management, managing accounts, shares management, short- and long-term investments, managing depreciable assets, raising capital (shares and loans).

- **Optional processes:** Procurement, Forex markets and currency conversion, international trade.
- **Frameworks and guidelines:** Relevant tax and accounting legislation, CPA, or equivalent guidelines.
- **Typical Customer:** The organisation (represented by the senior executive), the taxation office.
- **Stakeholders:** Everyone.
- **Work style:** Long-term planned work, suitable for planned Incremental Delivery.

The role of Finance and Accounting does not change dramatically under Agile Business Management. Changes are primarily to workflow and transparency.

Media and Communications

Media and Communications are responsible for interacting with the public, public relations, media press releases, brand awareness, and occasionally, social media.

- **Typical products:** Press releases.
- **Typical processes:** Press conferences, public relations.
- **Optional processes:** Social media interaction, corporate website.
- **Frameworks and guidelines:** N/A.
- **Typical Customer:** Sales and Marketing, senior executive, Delivery Teams.
- **Stakeholders:** External media.

- **Work style:** Mostly ad hoc, suitable for Continuous Delivery. Some project based (e.g. advertising campaigns), suitable for planned Incremental Delivery.

Under Agile Business Management, all staff share the responsibility of interacting with the public, especially when dealing with consumers, and the public, in the social media space. The role of Media and Communications in relation to brand and media affairs does not change dramatically. The standard changes to workflow and transparency apply to these Teams as well.

Legal

Legal support teams generally provide regulatory, liability, and indemnity advice, as well as draft, or review, contracts between the organisation and its Customers. In the extreme case, they will respond to legal action taken against the company.

- **Typical products:** Commercial contracts.
- **Typical processes:** Provide legal advice, ensure regulatory compliance, intellectual property management, overall risk management.
- **Optional processes:** Manage litigation, acquisitions and mergers.
- **Frameworks and guidelines:** Relevant legislation, bar association guidelines.
- **Typical Customer:** Sales and Marketing, senior executive, Delivery Teams.
- **Stakeholders:** Everyone.
- **Work style:** Advisory Requirements are generally ad hoc, suitable for Continuous Delivery. However, most

Requirements for the legal team are larger, and are suitable for Incremental Delivery.

The role of the Legal Department does not change dramatically under Agile Business Management. Like HR, changes are primarily to workflow, transparency and Customer interaction.

Research and Development

Research and Development (R&D) Teams are internally focused, and are responsible for improving existing products and services, as well as creating new ones.

- **Typical products:** Context specific. For example, a clothing producer may research faster production methods, new materials and new designs.
- **Typical processes:** N/A.
- **Optional processes:** N/A.
- **Frameworks and guidelines:** N/A.
- **Typical Customer:** Delivery Teams, senior executive.
- **Stakeholders:** Consumers (research), Finance and Accounting (forecasting and planning).
- **Work style:** Mid- to long-term planned work, suitable for planned Incremental Delivery.

While R&D's core responsibilities remain the same, under Agile Business Management, R&D products are delivered rapidly, and often in close alignment with the Delivery Teams. By empowering Delivery Teams to work closely with the Customer and consumers, you may be able to incorporate R&D responsibilities directly into the Delivery Teams.

Production and Operations – Delivery Teams

Generally, Production and Operations are the largest department in an organisation. Responsible for building core products, and/or delivering core services, Production and Operations are the reason your organisation exists.

> 📋 **Delivery Teams:** An internal department responsible for building core products, and/or delivering core services. Due to the highly variable range of responsibilities for Production and Operations Teams between organisations, Agile Business Management simplifies this by calling them all 'Delivery Teams'.

- **Typical products:** Context specific. For example, a clothing producer will produce clothing, and a financial services company will buy and sell shares for their clients.

- **Typical processes:** Materials procurement, resource scheduling, production cost management, production forecasts, quality control.

- **Optional processes:** Staff procurement, plant location and layout.

- **Frameworks and guidelines:** ISO9000, CMMI.

- **Typical Customer:** External clients, Sales and Marketing, product manager.

- **Stakeholders:** Everyone.

- **Work style:** Context specific. Can be ad hoc, suitable for Continuous Delivery, or long-term planned work; suitable for planned Incremental Delivery.

The majority of Agile Business Management changes occur within the Delivery (Production and Operations) Teams. These include greater Customer interaction, direct responsibility for delivery, and implementing Continuous or Incremental Delivery processes. In fact, most of the processes in this book apply to these Teams.

Other departments

This is by no means an exhaustive list of potential business functions or departments. Other departments can include; Project Management, Office Management, Facilities Management, Real Estate, Filing and Records Management, Secretariat, Business Intelligence, Libraries, etc. Applying the core Agile concepts and processes from this book, any department, or business function, can improve their agility, adaptability and engagement.

The Board and executive governance bodies

'The office of director ... a man ought not to fill without qualification.'

Lord Selborne, 1873

The governance of an organisation is more than just the management of its constituent departments. In larger organisations, oversight and overall governance sits with the Board of Directors, and through them, the CEO. As the company charter defines the Board's size, structure and administration, most organisations transitioning to Agile Business Management do not have the luxury of changing the Board.

However, for wide-scale adoption, the Board need to act as champions of Agile Business Management, and the same principles that govern the rest of the organisation, should govern them. Corporate objectives and policies set by the Board should be adaptable, iterative, testable, and able to take advantage of the dynamic marketplace. Measuring the performance of the organisation, and its CEO, should be based on Agile metrics (*see section: Managing Teams*) which, in turn, aligns executive remuneration with Agile KPIs.

The Board needs to be involved in the development of the Agile corporate strategies, and is responsible for monitoring the integrity, and effectiveness, of the Agile Business Management practices.

In addition to their legally binding responsibilities, Agile Boards need to apply greater due diligence to the governance of their organisation. This is not due to a lack of trust in their chosen executive, but because an Agile organisation can, and will, adapt and change rapidly. Because of this, the Board needs to work closely with the executive, to remain informed, so they can make appropriate governance decisions.

In order to deliver on their Agile obligations, the Board should expect greater transparency and communication from the organisation and the executive. This, in turn, improves their ability to act, in good faith, in the best interest of the organisation and its shareholders.

Management within an organisation is the responsibility of the CEO, although this is usually delegated to Department heads (*see section: Internal departments*), or specific executive governance committees. These executive committees provide oversight and guidance on complex issues within the organisation, and traditionally meet every two-three months for several hours, with 'out-of-session' meetings as required. Examples can include:

- **Investment committee:** Appointed (and usually chaired) by the CEO, the investment committee is responsible for approving major capital investment decisions across the organisation. By bringing stakeholders together, the investment committee reduces the risk of poor investment decisions.

- **Information management committee:** Appointed by the CEO or CIO, the information management committee is responsible for governing the information assets of the organisation. This highly complex issue often crosses Departmental bounds, so an expert committee can provide specialist advice and coordination.

- **Compensation committee:** Appointed by the Board of Directors, the compensation committee researches, and sets, the remuneration of the company's executive. This external committee reduces any perceived conflict of interest on this sensitive topic.

- **Project steering committee/working committee:** Ad hoc groups, created to oversee a specific project, event, or organisational issue.

Agile Business Management encourages the use of executive committees, to manage these complex issues for large organisations. They can be very effective as a mechanism for coordination and communication. However, like most other Agile processes, they should be fast, regular, and iterative.

For example, a traditional committee may meet every two months for four hours, whereas an Agile committee would meet every two weeks for one hour. Under this model, they meet for the same total duration, but with greater regularity, to take advantage of emerging business opportunities. Other characteristics of Agile meetings, as defined in section '*The Daily Stand-up and Agile meetings*', should apply to executive committees as well.

 Case study: New Zealand Post Group – An Agile executive!

New Zealand Post Group (NZPG) consists of a range of businesses, providing communication and business solutions to the New Zealand public and businesses, across all sectors and industries. Products and services range from the core mail business, through to banking and digital solutions.

NZPG, like many businesses after the global financial crisis, undertook a business review, and identified that there were a number of missed opportunities to respond to customer and market trends. It was realised that these opportunities would continue to be missed while the organisation was 'stuck' in old modes of operation.

In late 2011, the Group Leadership Team, consisting of the Group CEO, CFO, Group Heads and General Managers, began a transformation and continuous improvement programme, to improve the overall responsiveness of the organisation. This transformation led to the creation of the Sorting Room, a visualisation of the state of the organisation and its strategic initiatives, as well as related cultural and process changes.

This new approach to corporate strategy emphasised simplicity, visibility and trust, and ultimately changed the way the NZPG Executive operates.

The problems:

The need to be more responsive to changes in customer behaviour, and changes in the marketplace, was the primary stimulus for organisational transformation. Long feedback cycles were limiting the ability for the organisation to execute, and communicate, corporate strategy, which, in turn, limited its responsiveness.

Historically, the monthly executive board meetings were not effective at resolving organisational issues, or driving strategic change. These meetings usually lasted all day, with agendas filled with lengthy and unwieldy 'FYI' papers, that were often unrelated to the goals of the Group Leadership Team. The result was that participants would lose focus, and, after a certain point, 'the will to live'.

The rapidly changing business environment was the final catalyst for this transformation. This needed a new approach, where the focus was on solving problems from a group perspective, rather than the traditional siloed one.

The solution:

To address these problems, the Group General Manager of Innovation identified that the organisation needed a collaborative, problem-solving and decision-making environment, and so the 'Sorting Room' was born.

Drawing on Agile, Lean Six Sigma and Systems Thinking methods, the Sorting Room is a dramatic change in the way the Group Leadership Team operates. It is a central space that provides oversight of the strategic initiatives of the organisation, and it is reinforced with a weekly forum for the Group Leadership Team, to debate the strategic challenges facing the business, as well as emergent incidents and risks.

Each strategic initiative (such as revenue growth, business improvement and leadership) is allocated to an executive to champion. This person (and their group/division) is responsible for the delivery of the initiative, and the programmes of work underneath it. These programmes of work are rigorously monitored, and have strong gating processes, especially those programmes with large capital investment.

The weekly Sorting Room meeting starts by focusing on the impediments to success from across the business, particularly anything that affects staff. This is followed by the main agenda; an in-depth analysis into two of the strategic initiative programmes, by the relevant, responsible executive.

The Sorting Room meetings are not meant as a status report. It is an environment where the executive can share information and help each other. This means that if an in-depth analysis is put on the agenda, it is because the responsible executive has an issue to solve, and wants the help of their peers.

As a final step, the impact of each completed strategic initiative is measured against predefined metrics. These are an important part of the feedback loop, and ensure that the initiatives lead to quantifiable outcomes for the organisation.

Table 1: Differences between the old and new states

	Old state	New state
Environment	Boardroom	War room
Timeframes	Monthly (5-6 hours)	Weekly (2 hours)
Structure	Hierarchical	Flat (External facilitator)
Focus	FYI, Proposals	Problems, Questions
Pre work	Many papers	2 issues
Style	Written, Formal	Visual, Engaging
Ambience	Corporate	Informal
Criteria	Push	Pull
Visibility	Low	High

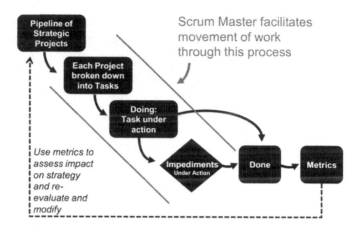

Figure 9: The Sorting Room workflow

The room itself contains a view of all the strategic initiatives, and associated work, across the organisation. There are five main areas to the room.

1 The Sorting Wall (Figure 10) is a Kanban Board that displays each strategic initiative across the wall. This is then split into the relevant stages; work that has started, work underway, impediments, and done. Attached to this is a listing of the key metrics (e.g. financial spend) for each of the strategic initiatives.

Figure 10: The Sorting Wall

2 The Scale Wall (Figure 11) provides a heat map
   of key activities across the top 10 strategic
   initiatives. By focusing on the programmes of
   work against time, the Scale Wall shows
   potential bottlenecks, and the impact of the
   initiatives on staff.

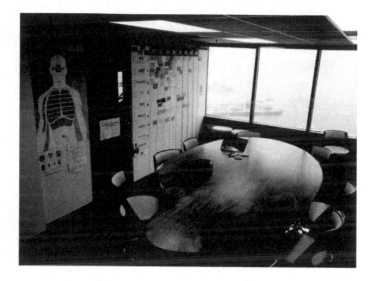

Figure 11: The Scale Wall

3　Next to the Scale Wall is a small information area, to remind the executive of the rules of the Sorting Room, what they are here to do, as well as general information, such as how much each meeting costs.

4　The final wall contains some clear working space for the topics under discussion.

5　Finally, there is a stylised elephant (Figure 12) on one wall, that represents 'the elephant in the room'. If anyone feels a topic is being ignored, or going unaddressed, they can attach a card to this wall, to raise it at the next Sorting Room meeting.

Figure 12: The elephant in the room

Each task on the Kanban Board is represented by a sticky note. Each note is colour coded according to the strategic aspect (e.g. people, process, customer, and finance) that the activity will affect. Additionally, to foster a culture of accountability, a photo of the responsible executive is attached to each note. This means that the Group Leadership Team can simply look at the wall, and determine the mix of impact across time, as well as who is responsible.

In order to promote a culture of transparency beyond the Group Leadership Team, the Sorting Room is available for anyone in the organisation to access and use. What has been found, is that teams will often use this room to hold their team meetings. The only difficulty this creates is that confidential, strategic initiatives have to use a code name, such as if the NZPG is doing a divestment or acquisition.

Finally, a senior manager within the organisation was selected to take on the responsibilities of the Executive Scrum Master. This person is responsible for facilitating the Sorting Room meetings, using an adapted Agile format, and utilising the above Kanban techniques. Given the sensitive nature of the Sorting Room meetings, it was important that the facilitator was somebody the Group Leadership Team could trust.

The implementation:

The Sorting Room was implemented in response to the challenge to find a better way to enhance collaboration between the Group Leadership Team in order to solve business problems, rather than the traditional 'boardroom' format. The challenge was accepted, and implemented, on one condition, they all agree to trial it, come what may, for at least six months.

It was important that the transformation was

effective, without being expensive. By leveraging internal talent, such as using the Business Improvement team to manage the implementation, and the design team to create colourful and appealing walls and plans, NZPG was able to implement the initial version of the Sorting Room and related processes within three weeks, with a minimal budget.

By engaging the Executive Scrum Master early on in the transformation process, the Group Leadership Team was guided through the new processes. This negated the need for any major training, beyond a brief introduction to the Sorting Room.

During the initial phase, the Head of Corporate Affairs was included, to communicate the changes across the organisation. They were responsible for broadcasting a monthly communiqué to all staff on what the 'Sorting Room' was, and the range of issues being addressed by the Group Leadership Team. The implicit message was: 'There is a new place and process to go through to get decisions from the Group Leadership Team, and it is very different from the previous format'.

The transformation itself adopted an iterative approach. The new processes were trialled based on a 'pure' Agile format, and then reviewed every six months to meet the current needs, and ways of working, of the Group Leadership Team.

Within the first six months, the Group Leadership Team was starting to realise the benefits of the Sorting Room. Through strong, robust conversations around strategy, there was greater visibility and collaboration between the executives, that, in turn, led to concrete actions being undertaken. By the end of 12 months, the Sorting Room had been enhanced to include focus on impediments, new visual cues on the Kanban Boards, as well as the new Scale Wall.

The challenges:

Initially, there was some resistance to the change, especially when the level of transparency became evident. The impact of having your photo attached to a post-it on a wall that anyone in the organisation could view, was powerful. This has led to the executives being significantly more open, and receptive, to being held accountable by their 'team'.

NZPG was also in the midst of changing from a federated business model, to a unified group. Therefore, the executive transformation also had to contend with the cultural lag associated with this organisational change.

Outside the executive, the only people who directly experienced this transformation were those presenting papers. Because of the shift in focus to problem solving, not all presenters received an easy ride. Those that were contributing to solutions had a more positive experience.

The outcomes:

Overall, the outcomes have been very positive, with substantial improvements compared to the original format. There are fewer FYI papers, and a greater focus on problem solving. There has been a tremendous impact on the level of collaboration, as the executive benefits from weekly meetings, and see each other far more frequently. There is a real sense that the executive are working as a team.

There has also been a noticeable difference in behaviours amongst the Group Leadership Team. The time estimations of actions have become more realistic, as has the substance of the actions. The executives are significantly more open, and receptive, to being held accountable by their 'team'.

The introduction of the Sorting Room has also had a pervasive effect on the wider organisational culture. There is a greater emphasis for the executives to work as a single team, rather than the traditional siloed approach. This has led to a greater understanding of each other's problems, and a collective ownership of responsibility.

Finally, the effect of going through the new process, and the associated level of visibility, has meant that this format has begun to be mimicked across the organisation.

The Sorting Room will continue to be optimised to get the best from the Group Leadership Team. Change takes time, even at executive level, and after the initial resistance by some, all are on board, and taking part in making the Sorting Room work.

- Paul Reid, Group GM Innovation, New Zealand Post Limited

- Jake Porterhouse, Executive Scrum Master, New Zealand Post Limited

Pair Work

> 'If you don't know where you are going, you will probably end up somewhere else.'

Lawrence J Peter, 1977

The concept of Pair Work draws directly from the Pair Programming technique, as defined by the Extreme Programming Agile development framework. In this technique, each Team member works as part of a pair, at a single workstation. Each person in the pair is either the 'Driver' or 'Observer', and has specific responsibilities. The Driver is responsible for doing the work, be that writing, developing, building, etc. The Observer is responsible for advising, and reviewing, the work. Each person in the pair switches roles frequently, usually about every 30 minutes, and they form new pairs each day. Figure 13 shows how each person in the pair changes throughout the process.

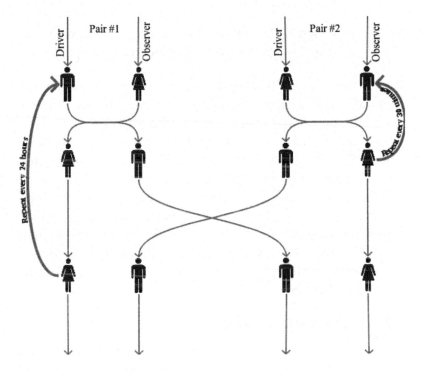

Figure 13: Pair Work flowchart

By separating the two responsibilities, the Driver can focus on developing the current Task as quickly as possible, whereas the Observer considers the bigger picture, and can suggest ideas for improvement, and identify likely, future problems. The act of observing improves discipline in the Team, both by reducing wasted time (e.g. surfing the web or checking e-mail) and improving attention to detail (e.g. writing supporting documentation, or recording outcomes). However, the major advantage of Pair Work is the overall reduction of defects created that need to be resolved later.

In general, Pair Work provides a major increase in quality, at the cost of a minor decrease in speed.

Whilst there are no formal studies in Pair Work outside the software engineering disciplines, several studies of Pair Programming have found that the quality of work significantly improves, compared to programmers working alone[2,3,4,5]. As well as improved design and maintainability, these studies show a reduction in defect rates between 15 and 50%, with a higher reduction in defect rates for high complexity Tasks, and using experienced pairs. While pairing, individual Tasks are generally completed sooner, however, overall development speed (including defect resolution), compared to programmers working alone, reduces by between 15-25%.

Pair Work example:

In this example, based on real-world Teams, two teams (of two people each) are working on the same tasks; Team 1 is using Pair Work and Team 2 is not.

Team 1 – Pair Work: Because Team 1 is using Pair Work they will work on Task A together and *then* Task B.

Task A	Initial Work	6 hours
	Testing	½ hour

2 *Evaluating Pair Programming with Respect to System Complexity and Programmer Expertise*, Arisholm, et al (Feb 2007).

3 *The Effect of Pairs in Program Design Tasks*, Lui, Chan and Nosek (Feb 2008).

4 *The Costs and Benefits of Pair Programming*, Cockburn and Williams (2000).

5 *Pair Programming Illuminated*, Williams and Kessler (2003).

	Rework	½ hour
	Defect Rate	2%
Task B	Initial Work	4 hours
	Testing	½ hour
	Rework	0 hour
	Defect Rate	4%
Overall	Total (Initial + Test + Rework)	(6+4) + (½+½) + (½+0) = 11.5 hours
	Average Defect	3%

Team 2 - Individual Work: Because Team 2 is not using Pair Work they are working on Task A and Task B *simultaneously*.

Task A & B	Initial Work	7 hours	6 hours
	Testing	1 hour	½ hour
	Rework	1 hour	1 hour
	Defect Rate	15%	10%
Overall	Total Max (Initial + Test + Rework)	(7) + (1) + (1) = 9 hours	
	Average Defect	12.5%	

You will notice that Team 1 took less time to deliver each Task, and had fewer defects. However, since they delivered Task A *then* Task B, they were slower overall than Team 2, who could deliver Task A and B at the same time (though they were still less accurate).

The value of Pair Work to your organisation will change between Requirements and Teams. As an Agile Manager, you need to compare the potential increase in quality and reduced dedicated testing time, against the increased overall time to deliver. This is not a rhetorical question, but a true judgement of value that you need to make, and verify, regularly.

Table 2: When to choose Pair Work

	Pair Work	VS.	**Individual Work**
Need	Quality driven		Speed driven
Type	Complex Tasks		Simplistic Tasks
Risk	High risk		Low risk
Team	Equal distribution of novices and experts		Low expert to novice ratio
Skills	Consolidated in one or two people		Cross-skilled Team Members

One of the key, qualitative advantages of Pair Work, is the implicit skills and knowledge transfer between partners. This includes both specific skills relating directly to the Task, and general knowledge transfer relating to work techniques and expertise. This is particularly valuable in the case of helping new employees to learn the standards and practices of the Team, and the specific Requirements of the current Customer. By switching partners each day, specific knowledge and skills quickly spread throughout the Team, promoting a cross-functional and cross-skilled Team.

Ultimately, Pair Work is a cooperative, social skill that requires good communication and trust between partners. This can be uncomfortable for Team Members unfamiliar with this process, and can take some time to learn. Regardless of organisational status or experience, both partners need to contribute equally, and listen to the other's ideas. Even as a mentoring mechanism, a new Team Member is still an equal partner in the pair.

As a final note, there is some controversy over the value of Pair Programming, and thus Pair Work. I leave it to you to decide if this approach will bring value to your organisation. At a minimum, however, I recommend that you apply Pair Work concepts to high-risk Tasks, and the training of new Team Members.

Team Facilitator

'A system must be managed. It will not manage itself.'

W Edwards Deming, 1993

The Team Facilitator is one of the most important roles within the Team. They are responsible for Team cohesion, building consensus, and ensuring that the Team understands, and follows, the Agile Business Management processes and values. Where appropriate, the Team Facilitator also tailors the Agile Business Management processes to meet the needs of the Team. The Team Facilitator should be experienced in Agile Business Management, and capable of teaching those skills to other Team Members, in order to improve the overall capability and skills of the Team. Facilitation is a difficult skill, and a good Team Facilitator needs to have specific characteristics to be successful.

- **Good people skills:** The Team Facilitator needs to be collaborative, with a good sense of humour, and provide a safe and constructive environment for the Team. This encourages Team cohesion, which, in turn, encourages higher morale and productivity.

- **Good communication skills:** Being able to stimulate discussion within the Team, and actively listen to each other's suggestions and feedback, is important for the Team Facilitator. This will reduce conflict, and provide an environment for creativity and innovation to flourish.

- **Good conflict resolution skills:** Team Facilitators need to be capable of resolving conflicting opinions between Team Members, while remaining neutral (but not passive) on the issues discussed, and assertive, without being overbearing. This will improve the overall effectiveness, and build an environment of trust, within the Team.

- **Knowledgeable but not necessarily an expert:** To be effective, the Team Facilitator needs to understand the work of all the Team Members. This ensures that the Team Facilitator can engage effectively with individual Team Members regarding their work, as well as understand the implications, and limitations, of new Requirements, or process changes, on the Team.

- **Fearless in removing impediments:** The Team Facilitator needs to be able to proactively stand-up for the Team, without fear or favour, when engaging with management, or other Teams. By quickly resolving impediments, the Team can be more productive, and deliver the Customers' Requirements faster, with minimal overhead.

- **Humble:** The Team Facilitator is a supporting role, only responsible to help the Team to be as effective as possible. While this role is important, the success and value comes from the entire Team (which they are a part of). This ensures that the Team benefits from the expertise of all Team Members, and that the Team Facilitator can be productive with their non-facilitation responsibilities.

- **Fostering curiosity and excitement:** Teams can get very busy dealing with day-to-day issues, and lose sight of the bigger picture. The Team Facilitator needs to provide context, to foster a sense of excitement within the team. The Team can be creative, make better long-term decisions, and enjoy their work. This, in turn, can improve the overall quality of their work.

- **Common sense:** The Team Facilitator needs to be able to apply common sense to the Team processes, rather than follow instructions blindly, and without thinking. This will ensure that the processes used by the Team meet the Team's specific needs.

- **Hands on:** Finally, the Team Facilitator is responsible for basic Team housekeeping, such as prepping materials, organising meetings, and ensuring that the Team has the tools to deliver the Customers' Requirements. This will ensure Team Members work effectively, and reduce their overhead when delivering Customer Requirements.

Finally, the Team Facilitator is *not* a command and control role, and should not be assigning Tasks, or making decisions for the team.

The Team Facilitator does not need to be the Team Leader, and in many cases, it can help if they aren't. Because the organisation imbues Team Leaders with institutional authority, Team Members will obey their instructions, regardless of any personal opinions. Agile Business Management is most effective when the Team buys-in to the process, and a Team Facilitator without institutional authority must build respect and trust in the Team, in order to get that buy-in.

Anyone familiar with Scrum, will recognise this role as similar to the Scrum Master.

 Team Facilitator: The person responsible for managing the Agile process within a Team. The Team Facilitator can be a Team Leader or Team Member.

Managing Teams

Q 'Treat your men as you would your own beloved sons. And they will follow you into the deepest valley.'

Sun Tzu, ~6th Century BCE

At this point, you have empowered your Teams to be accountable, and responsible, for their outcomes. This empowerment transfers many of the direct responsibilities for Customer engagement, Team management and planning, from the manager to the Team. Traditionally, the Team has always been responsible for delivery; empowerment just means that they have the direct authority to follow through. However, no matter how Agile or empowered your Teams are, you are still their manager. Whether direct or indirect, you still have responsibilities for their performance and their well-being.

If it isn't already obvious, Agile Business Management strongly emphasises the use of metrics, to understand, characterise, validate, and optimise the success, or otherwise, of the process. As part of the validation approach, you can use traditional Key Performance Indicators (KPIs) at each stage of the management process. This can help reduce the management overhead, and limit active management for productive Teams. You should assess Agile KPIs in the same context as the Agile work, this means that the KPIs should be Continuous or Incremental, automatable, and with a focus on Customer engagement.

Key Performance Indicator: A performance measurement to evaluate the success of a particular activity.

Standard KPI rules still apply. For example, they should be aligned to corporate strategic objectives, assigned to an individual or Team, actionable, easy to understand, a mixture of leading and lagging, and few in number.

KPIs used in your Team's, and staff performance management, need to include both quantitative and qualitative measures. Quantitative measures verify that the Team is delivering to specific Requirements, generally as defined by the Customers' Requirements Backlog. These are simple to measure, often drawn from a workload management system, and based on simple, numeric factors (such as the number of queries resolved). Qualitative measures verify that the Team is communicating well, and is fully engaged in planning, and working well together. These are difficult to measure directly, and are usually gathered through observation, and formal or informal feedback from colleagues.

 Quantitative KPIs:

- Are quality control tests occurring during every Iteration?

- Is the Team engaging with the Customer, or Customer Representative, regularly?

- Is the Customer, or Customer Representative, engaging with the Team regularly?

- Are Requirements being estimated, and consistently delivered?

- Are defects being resolved within two Iterations?

- Is there a reduction in identified defects by consumers (note: consumer, not Customer)?

- For Incremental Delivery, are 90% of planned and *estimated* Tasks being completed each Iteration (Velocity/goals achieved)?

- Have overhead costs (e.g. additional meetings,

delivery/release costs, delays) been reduced?

- Is the Team/person meeting *agreed* due dates?

Qualitative KPIs:

- Are Retrospectives being effectively utilised?
- Is the Customer happy with the work being produced?
- Is the Iteration planning accurate?
- Peer review, or 360° review (controversial, but often effective)?

 Velocity: The rate of delivery of Requirements per Iteration, or other fixed period.

Two examples of metrics that you should monitor, yet make poor KPIs, are the accuracy of estimates, and the percentage of Quality Control Tests that pass. KPIs based on passing early Quality Control Tests promote poor quality control, as failing tests are both expected, and provide, positive feedback to the Team. Similarly, estimation accuracy is impacted by a large number of factors, many of which the Team have no control over.

Collecting, and measuring, metrics without organisational awareness and acceptance for the rationale behind them, can lead to some Team Members manipulating their outcomes, purely to meet metrics or KPI targets. In these situations, collecting metrics can actually cause significant harm, and can lead to a complete failure of business process. Staff need to be aware that metrics and KPIs are used to improve outcomes and discover business process issues, not to assign blame.

Agile specific KPIs are valid regardless of whether they are standalone, or part of a balanced scorecard[6] approach.

Under an Agile Business Management model, your staff need to undertake continuous professional development, to remain effective and competitive. Professional development can take many forms, from formal external training, attending conferences, pairing (or mentoring) with senior staff, or working across different Teams. The cross-functional Teams themselves promote ongoing skills-transfer between Team Members. As part of being empowered, individuals need to be responsible for identifying, and obtaining, their own professional development needs.

Managing Distributed Teams

'A leader leads by example not by force.'

Sun Tzu, ~6th Century BCE

In modern business, geographically distributed Teams are becoming significantly more common. Reasons for distributing your Team might include the availability of resources in different locations, closeness to certain business or technology clusters, proximity to Customers, or cost advantages. With a bit of common sense, and some minor adjustments to the process, it is simple to run Agile Business Management with geographically distributed Teams.

---

6 *The Balanced Scorecard: Translating Strategy Into Action*, Kaplan and Norton (1996).

The same core rules apply to Team creation as with co-located Teams. To ensure a successful Team, only recruit self-motivated and highly skilled staff. Though it may take longer to create the Team, weak Team Members may be unable to cope with a lack of direct management, and will hamper delivery. If you must use less skilled Team Members, make sure they work from the office, where you, or other managers, can closely manage them, and only use the best Team Members for remote work.

By distributing your Team Members, you run the risk of poor Team cohesion, which, if you remember from the start of this chapter, will reduce efficiency, and can reduce many of the benefits of Agile Business Management. To mitigate this risk, make additional effort to ensure that all Team Members feel responsible, and accountable, for the achievement of the overall goal, whereby nobody can succeed without everybody else being successful. This will help foster a sense of teamwork and staff loyalty. If possible, supplement this by regularly swapping Team Members between geographic locations, allowing people to meet face to face, promote skills transfer, and improve their professional relationships.

While multiple Teams can be easily distributed, where possible, all members in a single Team should be co-located. It is easier to manage and coordinate distributed Teams, rather than distributed Team Members. Don't take this as an excuse to be lazy, and design a Team based on the skills at hand; form Teams around the *required* skills, not around the *available* skills.

Lastly, communication is the key to any successful delivery, especially in distributed Teams. You must set up, and enforce, a communications process early in the work cycle that includes:

- Invest in regular face-to-face meetings, especially when forming a new Team. This ensures that the Team Members get to meet their colleagues, share skills, and build strong, working relationships.

- Encourage the use of multiple technologies (such as e-mail, online chat, tele/video conferencing, and social media) to encourage regular, and effective, communication. By providing different communication platforms, individual Team Members can choose the most appropriate channel for a given conversation.

- Where appropriate, record, and retain, all formal communication, for future reference. Written communication (such as e-mail) is easier to search than voice or video. This provides a location where Team Members can easily refer to decisions and discussions on Requirements or technical issues. However, be aware that the communication value of e-mail is significantly lower than that of other communication channels.

- Invest in professional video conferencing hardware for each major centre, and ensure that all individual Team Members have basic video conferencing functionality at their workstations. Overall, communication improves when participants are able to see non-verbal cues.

Remember Agile principle #6: The most efficient and effective method of conveying information to, and within, a development team, is face-to-face conversation.

Risk management

'Fall seven times. Stand up eight.'

Old Japanese Proverb

As work in an Agile organisation is continuously adapting to meet changing business needs, aggressive risk and issue management is an important governance outcome. Project managers will be familiar with many of these concepts, as Agile Business Management applies the same risk and issue management rigour from project management, to all areas of corporate management.

Risk: A risk is something (generally negative) that could happen, and is assessed in terms of likelihood and potential impact.

Issue: An issue is an event, change or risk that has occurred, or is occurring.

A risk can apply to any part of your organisation, and can either be a business, technical, or resource risk. Business risks apply to areas of your business, such as corporate processes, financial management (e.g. cashflow), or Customer engagement (e.g. satisfaction). Technical risks apply to your Production and Operations Teams, and relate to the delivery of Customer Requirements. Resource risks apply to staff management, and can be in areas, such as unexpected absences (e.g. late to work, sick leave, death, etc.), delays in recruitment, skill gaps, or fraud.

The likelihood, and impact, of some risks may change by using Agile Business Management over traditional management frameworks. For example:

Higher risks

- Impact due to no Customer buy-in
- Impact due to poor support by secondary functions (such as HR)
- Likelihood of scope change

Lower risks

- Impact due to rework
- Likelihood of poor estimation
- Impact due to scope change

Teams are responsible for identifying and managing risks, however, as an Agile Manager, you need to regularly monitor, and assess, these risks. Each risk should describe what could happen, how it may happen, when it may happen, the likelihood of it happening, the impact if it happens, and how it can be avoided or mitigated (treatment). It is important to remember that each risk may have more than one cause and treatment.

Where possible, base likelihood and impact on quantitative measures, such as financial, and schedule impact or historical percentile likelihood. Poor logic, insufficient evidence, and even plain old wishful thinking, can significantly bias qualitative measures, such as the traditional high/low rating.

Four basic techniques apply in the management and treatment of risks.

1 **Avoid:** A Team can avoid a risk by not performing the work that leads to it. Examples may include; not holding a meeting because a Team Member is sick and you don't

want to spread the illness, to not driving to work because you may have an accident on the way. The disadvantage to avoiding a risk is that you also miss the benefits.

2 **Reduce:** A Team can reduce the impact, or likelihood, of a risk, by changing the work that causes the risk, or putting in place alternative activities. Examples may include; additional investment in communications tools for distributed Team Members before commencing work for a Customer, or co-locating all Team Members to a single location close to the Customer. The disadvantage of reducing a risk is the additional cost required to implement the reduction strategy.

3 **Share:** A Team can share a risk by outsourcing, or insuring, the work required for a Customer. Examples may include; acquiring public liability insurance to protect against accidents in the workplace, to acquiring professional indemnity insurance to protect against civil lawsuits. The disadvantage of sharing a risk is the additional cost involved, and the legal disagreements that can occur when the shared risk does not exactly correlate to the contractual arrangements.

4 **Retain:** A Team can retain (or accept) a risk if they are willing to accept the impact of the risk should it occur. Examples may include; purchasing incorrect office supplies, as the cost to replace is very low; to a terrorist attack, as the likelihood is so low, and the cost to mitigate is very high. The obvious disadvantage of retaining a risk is that there is no strategy in place if the risk occurs, and it has a greater impact than expected.

Example risks:

Risk #1

- *Risk:* Poor Customer engagement
- *Caused by:* Conflict between a Team Member and Customer
- *Likelihood:* Low
- *Impact:* High
- *Treatment:* Provide formal induction for all staff in Agile processes. Provide ongoing support and training in communication skills
- *Likelihood after treatment:* Very low
- *Impact after treatment:* Medium

Risk #2

- *Risk:* Negative product reviews
- *Caused by:* Dissatisfied consumers who purchased our product
- *Likelihood:* High
- *Impact:* Very low
- *Treatment:* Additional quality control in product development and training for help desk staff
- *Likelihood after treatment:* Moderate
- *Impact after treatment:* Very low

Risk #3

- *Risk:* Data loss
- *Caused by:* ICT systems crash
- *Likelihood:* 0.5% per year

- *Impact:* $500,000
- *Treatment:* Creating mirrored systems and off-site back-up
- *Likelihood after treatment:* Very low
- *Impact after treatment:* Moderate

Risk #4

- *Risk:* Production system outage
- *Caused by:* ICT systems crash
- *Likelihood:* 1.8% per year
- *Impact:* $50,000
- *Treatment:* Redundant production systems with regular disaster recovery and business continuity tests
- *Likelihood after treatment:* Very low
- *Impact after treatment:* Low

Risk #5

- *Risk:* Property damage
- *Caused by:* Fire, flood, etc.
- *Likelihood:* Very low
- *Impact:* $15,000,000
- *Treatment:* Business continuity insurance
- *Likelihood after treatment:* Very low
- *Impact after treatment:* Moderate

Once identified, risks are recorded in the Team's Risk Register, which in true Agile fashion, is visible to all stakeholders. Record each risk in the Risk Register separately, even related risks, to support the needs of different Teams. Teams can manage very low, low, and medium risks, internally, but need to report high, and very high risks, even if they can manage them internally.

 Risk Register: A log of all risks for a specific Team and Customer.

You do not need to treat, or monitor, all risks, as treating risks costs time and money. You need to decide what level of risk you are willing to accept (your risk appetite), and how much you are willing to invest in avoiding risks you can't accept.

As a final word, there are many good books on the subject of risk, and risk management, that will provide detail[7], and, in some cases, guidelines[8] on implementing good risk management.

---

7 *Waltzing With Bears: Managing Risk on Software Projects*, DeMarco and Lister (2003).

8 *The Black Swan: The Impact of the Highly Improbable*, Taleb (2007).

CHAPTER 4: WORK, THE AGILE WAY

💬 'Opportunity is missed by most people because it is dressed in overalls and looks like work.'

Thomas Edison, ~1900

Aim of this chapter: To provide business managers with the tools and techniques needed to optimise workflow, exploit change, and manage Customer Requirements in an adaptable and flexible way. Based on proven Agile and lean processes, and aligned to the Agile philosophy, these techniques cover the full work-cycle, through planning, design, development, quality control, to completion.

At this point, after examining the role of the Customer and Team, it's time to get to work. Work, the Agile way, is defined as the sum of Requirements made by a single Customer to a Team, or related group of Teams, and delivered in an Incremental, or Continuous, manner. Depending on the context, and Customer's Requirements, there could be anywhere between an hour, to a decade's work.

📋 **Work:** The sum of Requirements made by a single Customer to a Team, or related group of Teams, and delivered in an Incremental, or Continuous, manner.

Prior to work commencing, and as described in section *Requirements and the Requirements Backlog*, your Customer creates the initial vision (or business case), and ordered Requirements Backlog (a regularly updated list of Customer Requirements). This vision provides the context of the end goal, and the Backlog helps your Teams to understand what they will be delivering, in the short to medium term. Teams analyse, plan, and design their work, based on this Backlog, and, unlike traditional methods, the full Team should undertake initial analysis. As the Requirements Backlog changes regularly, to reduce wasted effort the Teams keep high-level analysis and planning to a minimum, and this should never take more than 1% of the total estimated duration (e.g. 2.5 days effort for 12 months work).

Q   Remember Agile value #2: We value [**completed Customer Requirements**] over comprehensive documentation.

Work is traditionally undertaken in one of two ways; business-as-usual and project based. Business-as-usual work is ongoing, continuous, and generally low risk. Whereas project-based work is temporary, with clear start and end dates, defined benefits (though benefits under Agile frameworks are not always defined), and generally utilising formal project management frameworks, such as PRINCE2®, PMBoK or Scrum.

Agile Business Management changes this, by providing two sets of processes for undertaking work, based on size and complexity; these are Continuous Delivery and Incremental Delivery. Continuous Delivery is best for small, discrete, self-contained, and generally repetitive Requirements. You should be able to deliver the majority of these in a few hours, to a few days of effort, in the order defined in the Requirements Backlog. Many traditional business-as-usual responsibilities fall under Continuous Delivery; however, you can deliver some traditional projects in this manner. Figure 14 shows a simple, continuous flowchart; where the delivery cycle takes new Customer Requirements from the Backlog, then releases the Completed Requirement to the Customer, before proceeding to the next.

Help desk support is generally Continuous in nature. Issues are raised as identified, and the related work can usually be resolved very quickly.

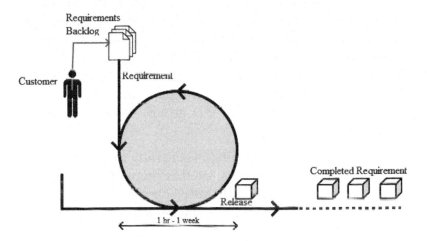

Figure 14: Simple continuous process flowchart

Remember Agile principle #3: Deliver working software [completed Requirements] frequently, from a couple of weeks, to a couple of months, with a preference to the shorter timescale.

Incremental Delivery is required when delivering complex groups of Requirements that require a large investment in time to complete, usually a few weeks to a few months.

Assigning Requirements into identically sized and managed Iterations for delivery, ensures that you can meet your Customer's needs regularly and accurately. Each Iteration is between one-four weeks, at the end of which the Team delivers a functional, self-contained, tested, and usable, though incomplete, outcome.

The product itself will continue to evolve, as each Iteration builds upon the last. The product is only 'complete' at the end of the last Iteration. The majority of traditional project-based work should be delivered Incrementally, however, many complex business-as-usual functions could also be delivered in this way. Figure 15 shows a simple, incremental flowchart; where the delivery cycle takes a group of Customer Requirements, which forms the Iteration Backlog, then, after a predetermined time, releases the Completed Requirements in this group, before proceeding to the next group.

Financial Management is generally Incremental in nature. Requirements, such as preparing budgets or annual reports, are identified early, take several weeks to complete, and can be delivered in smaller Iterations.

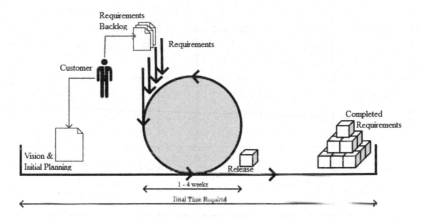

Figure 15: Simple incremental process flowchart

Table 3: When to use Continuous or Incremental Delivery

	Continuous	vs.	Incremental
Effort	Hours to days		Weeks to years
Notice	On-demand (no notice)		Planned
Deliver	Single requirements		Multiple Requirements with multiple tasks
Backlog	Requirements Backlog		Requirements Backlog and Iteration Backlog

Change	Constantly changing Requirements Backlog		Fixed Iteration Backlog
Release	On-demand per Requirement		End of each Iteration (multiple Requirements)
Planning	On-demand per Requirement		Start of each Iteration (multiple Requirements)
Kanban	Requirement Cards		Task Cards

Benefits of the Agile Business Management work model include:

- Repeatable and generic estimation techniques that aid in workload management and Iteration Planning.

- By comparing estimates against actuals, you can build a known rate of delivery (Velocity) which improves forward planning.

- Reduced overtime through easily measurable and estimatable work, with accurate work planning. Do not mistake this for the ability to do more in the same time.

- Higher quality outcomes through embedded quality control processes.

- Simplification of overall work, by focusing on immediate, short-term Requirements.

- Greater Customer satisfaction through early, regular and targeted delivery.

To control and visualise the flow of Tasks, both delivery mechanisms use a pipeline Agile technique called Kanban, covered in section *Kanbans*.

The overhead of managing all these Requirements and Tasks can be quite daunting. However, there are multitudes of workload management systems available to help track and manage them. A good, workload management system will also become the de-facto knowledge base, containing all information regarding each Requirement and its delivery. This can help in the development, or resolution, of similar requests.

- Link the workload management system with HR and ERP systems to bill Customers and/or pay contractors.

- If kept up to date, the workload management system can then be used as a reporting tool, to assess progress.

- Provide direct access to Customers, so they can communicate directly with the Team, and take part in quality control processes.

Tools are important to simplify the process, but are just a means to an end. Remember, back in the *Introduction*, the first point of the Agile Manifesto was 'We value **individuals and interactions** over processes and tools'. A tool is effective only if the investment in using the tool, such as staff time, is less than the cost of not using the tool, or using a simpler tool. As a rule, your Team Members should spend no more than 10 minutes a day using any workflow management system.

Case study: WIKISPEED – Applying Agile software principles and practices for fast automotive development![1]

WIKISPEED: The WIKISPEED SGT01 car was an entrant in the Progressive Insurance Automotive X Prize contest, to produce a full-sized, road-legal car, getting 100+ mi/gal (2.25L/100 km). Agile methods were introduced, to give product cycle times measured in weeks, not years.

This case study describes how a distributed, collaborative team of volunteers, spread around the world, is creating, on a shoestring budget, a model for how to design and manufacture a highly efficient automobile. WIKISPEED is doing this by borrowing, and evolving, concepts from a variety of sources, such as Agile and lean software development, and continuing to evolve them in order to fit the context of automobile research, design and production. In particular, WIKISPEED is adapting aspects of Agile software development principles and practices to the research, design and production of physical products.

The solution

Borrowing processes from Extreme Programming and Scrum, WIKISPEED has created a research, design and production cycle, in which changes can be made to any part of the automobile, every week. These Agile principles and practices have resulted

---

1 *Applying Agile Software Principles and Practices for Fast Automotive Development,* Socha, Folsom and Justice (2012).

in several innovations, including:

- A highly modular automobile.
- A lightweight (68kg) aluminium load bearing chassis, with high crash protection.
- A low-cost process to create the car's composite aeroshell, without metal stamping, moulds or autoclaves.
- A fuel-efficient engine control unit we call WIKISPEEDlet.

The implementation

Good Agile design demands modules that are loosely coupled, and can be tested apart from the entire system. These principles have led to a modular automotive design. On the WIKISPEED car, major sub-assemblies, such as suspension, motor, and body, can be replaced in the time it takes to change a flat tyre. The wheels and suspension bolt to the chassis, and can be repositioned or replaced. The composite body bolts to the chassis (Figure 16), and allows exchange of external shells. The same car can be a race car today, and a pick-up truck tomorrow.

Figure 16: WIKISPEED – Chassis

This modularity supports many of our design and process principles. It allows for rapid Iterations and experimentations during development and testing. Loosely coupled components, with simple and well-defined interfaces, minimise system interdependencies, enabling more rapid and reliable software and hardware development. Modularity allows unit tests of individual systems, and supports concurrent engineering and experimentation. It leads to more innovation, which contributes to low design costs, low manufacturing cost, more long-term evolution, and more consumer post-sale options.

The challenges

To minimise weight, we wanted to use a structural carbon fibre body; however, the lowest bid of $36,000 over three months (with waived labour costs) was beyond our budget, especially when factoring in changes during each Iteration. To overcome this, Robert Mohrbacher (one of our team members) pioneered a composites process that takes considerably less time and money to go from a CAD drawing to a full, structural carbon fibre body. This process now only requires $800 for materials, and only takes three days; these significant savings in capital and time allow us to more quickly experiment and adapt.

The outcomes

Figure 17: WIKISPEED – SGT01 car as of January 2011, at the North American International Auto Show

Based upon over two years of WIKISPEED experience, we summarise what has been important to date, and what might be applicable to other projects. The following were critical to the WIKISPEED project:

- (Joe Justice's) persistently enthusiastic leadership.
- Borrowing, and evolving, principles and

practices from Agile software development, Extreme Programming, lean manufacturing, etc.

- Having access to little capital.

The term 'Extreme Programming' was coined because the authors of that process combined 13 good practices, to reap a synergistic result. The set of practices described in this paper may be the beginning of a similar set that could be called 'Extreme Manufacturing'.

WIKISPEED is pioneering a qualitatively different approach to the research, design and production of automobiles. It has long been known that the Waterfall Method does not work well with software, where requirements are unknowable and subject to rapid change. Lean product design and manufacturing both take a much more iterative approach to this work for physical products. WIKISPEED is trying to push this even further, largely by applying software design principles and practices to automotive engineering. Our experience indicates that this can dramatically speed up the automotive development time, reduce the need for expensive tooling, and potentially lead to a qualitatively different business model.

- David Socha, University of Washington Bothell

- Tyler C Folsom, QUEST Integrated Inc.

- Joe Justice, Team WIKISPEED

Phases of delivery

'Sometimes you just have to jump out the window and grow wings on the way down.'

Ray Bradbury, 1995

Both Continuous and Incremental Delivery have four key phases: Planning, Do, Review and Release. Continuous Delivery will cycle through these phases for each Requirement, whereas Incremental Delivery will cycle through these for each Iteration.

 Planning: The process of determining the target scope of delivery and (if appropriate) defining the Iteration Backlog.

 Do: The process of actively working on the Requirements.

 Review: The (formal or informal) process of verifying that the completed Requirement meets the Customer's expectations, and accepting them for Release.

Release: The process of delivering completed Requirements to the Customer.

Your business process model for the four phases may look a little like Figure 18.

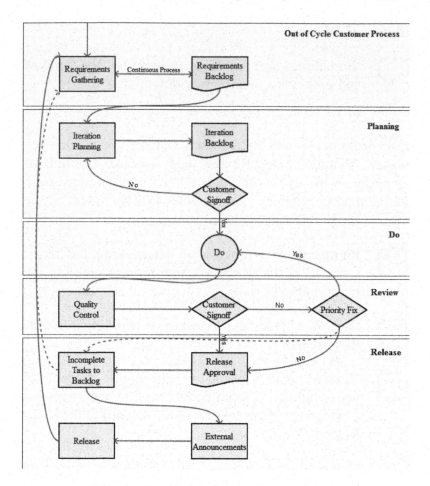

Figure 18: Business process flowchart

Planning phase

Contrary to common opinion, it is important to have a good understanding of the expected outcomes, before starting work on any Agile Requirement. This is the goal of the Planning phase, and provides a forum for your Customer and Teams to discuss the needed Requirements. This step in the process focuses on determining the target scope of delivery, and, for Incremental Delivery, defines the Iteration Backlog. The Customer, or Customer Representative, is responsible for ensuring the Requirements Backlog is up to date, in preparation for the Planning phase. This includes clarification and reordering of the Customer Requirements, with consideration of any inherited, or incomplete, Requirements.

For Incremental Delivery, the Planning phase should take no longer than two hours per week. This can be adjusted pro-rata for longer Iterations, e.g. four hours for two weeks, and eight hours for four weeks. At the end of the Planning phase, the Team should have an estimated, ordered, and detailed Iteration Backlog, based on the Customers' Requirements.

Remember Agile principle #9: Continuous attention to technical [and non-technical] excellence and good design enhances agility.

There are two stages to the Planning phase, business and technical specifications. The business specification of the Planning phase aims to, with your Customer, select the highest priority Requirements from the Requirements Backlog, and turn them into a realistic goal. This also provides your Customer with the opportunity to communicate the required scope of delivery, provide the business context and priority, and address any questions the Team may have, to assist with performing the solution decomposition and estimation steps.

Distribute a copy of the Requirements Backlog prior to the Planning phase, to provide the Team with time to consider solution options for discussion during the workshop, and prepare clarification questions for the Customer.

The second part of the Planning phase is technical, and, though they do not need to be physically present, the Customer must be available to the Teams, to discuss issues and answer questions. This is the solution design and estimating step in the Planning process, and aims to determine how to deliver each Requirement, by breaking it into its composite Tasks. The Team is also responsible for estimating the effort for all the Tasks in the Requirements, and (optionally) writing the Quality Control Test-Cases. This process of solution decomposition may reveal additional, or more complex, Tasks, that were not apparent during the high-level Planning. In this situation, the Customer must be available to review and approve if the agreed scope of the Iteration needs to change.

Each Task should take no longer than four-eight hours of effort to complete, and there will usually be multiple Tasks per Requirement.

Figure 19 describes the general flow of activity in this step.

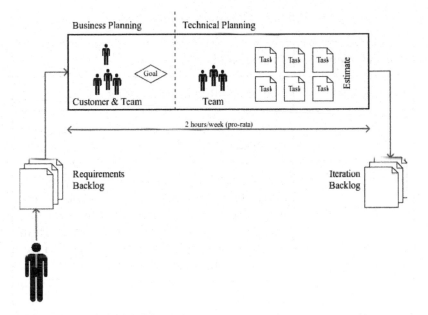

Figure 19: Work Planning

As a guideline, large Tasks should be broken into Tasks preferably no longer than one day, and Tasks that involve waiting, split into separate Tasks (pre-wait and post-wait). This enables accurate tracking, and the calculation of Velocity (*see section: Measuring progress*). For complex Requirements, or those with a high number of interdependencies, it may be necessary to split the Task decomposition and estimating activities into two, and allow your Team Members an opportunity to consult with external parties on feasibility, and obtain input into the estimating process.

Always remember that only the Team can create Tasks, but only the Customer can create Requirements.

Table 4: Components of a task

Task elements	Description
Requirement	The parent Requirement of the Task.
Task summary	One sentence that briefly describes, and identifies, the Task.
Owner	The person who selects the Task, and is accountable for delivering it. The owner may change at any point in the Iteration, especially as it changes state (e.g. from Active to Testing). However, one person can only own the Task at a time (unless using Pair Work, in which case a 'pair' will own it).
Estimate	The estimate in hours is the amount of effort the Team agrees is required to complete the specified Task. The estimate includes Planning, Do, Review, Release, and additional documentation.

- Prepare beforehand.
- Planning is a creative, problem-solving process. Encourage brainstorming.
- Ensure the Planning room has plenty of paper, a whiteboard, and a computer with Internet access.

Do phase

The activities within the Do phase are Team specific. In general, the Team works through each Task in a Requirement, with the aim of delivering all the completed Requirements at the end of the Iteration.

Review phase

At the stage when the Team is expected to Release to the Customer (e.g. once an Iteration is nearly Complete), the Requirements selected by the Customer and Team are either 'Done' or 'Not Done'. 'Done' Requirements are those where all the prerequisite Tasks associated with it are also 'Done'. Incomplete or 'Not Done' Tasks are reviewed in the context of the Requirements that they belong to, and if it affects whether the Requirement can be considered Done. If the Requirement can still be delivered, any remaining 'Not Done' Tasks may be rolled into a new Requirement for the next Iteration, or discarded if no longer required, in which case the current Requirement is considered Done.

Following Agile principles, your Customer is responsible for the Review phase, and will examine, test, and, if satisfied, accept a Requirement is Done. This can either be a formal review and User Acceptance Testing process, or an informal review and sign off. Either way, the Customer needs to engage with the Team, by providing ongoing feedback, and regularly updating the Requirements Backlog.

 Sign off: The formal approval that a Requirement has been completed to the Customer's satisfaction.

In order to properly manage expectations, and ensure acceptance of the Requirement, it is critical that management, Customers, and the Teams, all have the same definition of 'Done'. Components of a Requirement may include analysis, documentation, and/or quality control, so to be 'Done', the Team must complete these secondary Tasks. If, at the end of an Iteration, a Task or Requirement is functionally complete but not 'Done', your Customer must be made aware, and the outstanding work returned to the Requirements Backlog for reordering. As a rule, your Customer should not expect to review Requirements that are 'Not Done'.

Remember Agile principle #10: Simplicity, the art of maximising the amount of work not done, is essential.

Release phase

The Release phase is where the completed Requirements are delivered to your Customer, and depends on the context; large, complex or single Customer Requirements, tend to use Incremental Delivery, and Release once at the end of the Iteration, whereas multi-Customer or standalone Requirements tend to Release as each Requirement is Done. Organisations that have a central Release process, outside the Teams control, can Release in larger blocks (e.g. quarterly). However, it is important that the Customer has access to the completed Requirements for review as early as possible, regardless of how late the Release will be.

Finally, your Teams can still Release Requirements that meet the Definition of Done, but have outstanding minor defects or features. These outstanding defects or Tasks accrue in the Requirements Backlog as 'Technical Debt'; which, while not Customer Requirements, still need to be ordered and planned like any other Requirement. Your Teams should address Technical Debt on a regular basis, to ensure manageable, and high-quality, outcomes. The Customer also needs to be aware of the impact on their Requirements, if the Team is never given the opportunity to address the Technical Debt. I recommend that you allocate a fixed percentage of your Team's time, negotiated with the Team and Customer, to address Technical Debt.

Technical Debt: Technical 'Requirements' in the Requirements Backlog that are not direct requests from the Customers, but are needed to improve overall quality of the product or service.

If a Team is unable to complete the non-critical Task, such as minor documentation for a Requirement, it is returned to the Requirements Backlog with a note, 'Finish documentation for Requirement X', and (probably) assigned to the next Iteration.

Case Study: Suncorp – Agile and Internal Audit!

The Suncorp Group provides general insurance, banking, life insurance, superannuation and investment services, across Australia and New Zealand. Within the Group, the Internal Audit Department assists Suncorp's Board, and Management achieve their objectives by independently evaluating and reporting on the effectiveness of risk management, controls and governance processes. Internal Audit engages with all levels and areas across the Group, and is accountable to the Suncorp Board.

The problems:

The key challenge facing the Internal Audit department was delivering on a large portfolio of complex audits, within a dynamic environment. This was compounded by the challenge of managing a team of people across several locations who are working on multiple projects across six portfolios, while ensuring effective information sharing.

It was difficult to ascertain transparency of individual audit progress, and visibility of the delivery of the overall, annual audit plan. Audits that were impacted by similar issues were difficult to identify, and unable to leverage off each other in terms of common solutions.

The solution:

The proposal to use Agile practices within the Internal Audit department was inspired by the very projects that were being audited. As the majority of projects at Suncorp are delivered using Agile, the Internal Audit department took many of these practices, and began to apply them internally. For example:

- **The regular Stand-up:** Holding a weekly Stand-up meeting provided a regular opportunity to reflect on the team's progress towards delivering the Audit Plan. It is a forum to discuss each audit: what was achieved during the past seven days, to set goals for the next seven days, and to highlight any risk, blockers or challenges.

- **Burndown Charts**: The use of Burndown Charts to measure, and report, on progress, helped shift the mentality to value delivered, rather than time spent.

- **Retrospectives**: These replaced the traditional post-implementation review of audits, as well as some aspects of the individual performance reviews after audit jobs. Retrospectives now include auditees as well, to support creation of a continuous learning and improvement culture within the team.

- **Kanban Boards**: Central to the use of Agile within Internal Audit, the physical 'Journey Board' is a visual representation of how the team is progressing on the delivery of the Annual Audit Plan. It provides a means for the whole team to review the status of Internal Audit's progress overall, at a team, portfolio and individual level.

Where appropriate, these practices were refined, to ensure they aligned to audit processes, while remaining true to the Agile principles.

The physical Journey Board defines the four states that each audit passes through, for example; Planning, Fieldwork, Response and Final. To move from one state to the next requires that the audit meet clearly defined deliverables, called 'Toll Gates'. In order to reinforce these deliverables, the

Toll Gates, and associated criteria, are physically printed on the Journey Board. Audits can only be moved through these Toll Gates during the stand-up, which is important to ensure appropriate rigour in the audit process.

The Toll Gates between states are as follows:

1. **Planning to Fieldwork:** Purpose of Audit defined through focusing questions, and agreed with audit team and auditees. Entrance meeting held, and Audit underway.

2. **Fieldwork to Response:** Workpapers completed, exit meeting held, and draft report sent.

3. **Response to Final:** Final report sent and retrospectives completed.

To measure progress, each time an audit passes through a 'Toll Gate', it accrues points, based on the number of days assigned to the Audit, weighted by the gate passed. This measure of velocity can be visualised on the Burndown Charts, and can then be broken down into points per portfolio, and points per Audit Leader.

The implementation:

The adoption of Agile practices was relatively smooth, as there was already a culture of Agile emerging across the Suncorp Group. In this environment, it was initially decided to minimise the use of formal training, and rely on experience, and experimentation, to drive the understanding of Agile within the team, and use the wisdom of the crowd by leveraging the project team resources audit works with.

The transition was led by a core of 'champions' who were responsible for creating the initial Agile environment, and adjusting it as required. The team took a relatively direct approach to the transition:

1. The first step was to implement the process changes, e.g. the 'Journey Board', approximately 100 audits for the year were installed overnight, by a few enthusiastic team members.

2. This led, naturally, to changing the way the team reported on the progress of audits, through the use of burndown charts.

3. Finally, with the process changes underway, many of the cultural changes could be implemented. For example, the way in which the department recognised the achievements of the auditors and teams, and fostering a culture where it is OK to call out blockers/challenges, and ask for assistance of the team where required.

Over time, the new audit processes have continued to evolve, as the team learnt what worked and what didn't.

The challenges:

It was recognised early on that effectively embedding Agile principles into the way the team worked, required a cultural change. Most of the audits undertaken had fixed constraints, such as budgeted time, and fixed 'Toll Gates' imposed on them. The trick was being Agile within these constraints (and knowing what the constraints were). The approach to this was to create, and communicate, a hybrid between 'old' expectations and structures, and the new.

The criteria that needed to be met to pass each of the Journey Board Toll Gates, were originally very detailed. This made the process complex and confusing, especially during the transition to agile practices. To resolve this, the number of criteria on each Toll Gate was reduced to one or two, focusing on the deliverables required at each Toll Gate.

While there were many auditors who were enthusiastic about the transition to Agile, some had heard incorrect comments that Agile meant removing the need for budgets, and other fixed constraints. Others were wary, and felt that this approach was inappropriate for Internal Audit, or trivial.

Although artefacts, such as story walls and burn-up charts, were introduced, there was an initial period where auditors were uncomfortable in using these artefacts to manage their audits, or with raising issues and blockers in front of their peers at stand-ups. This was overcome by walking the talk, i.e. demonstrating open communication, and the benefits of flexible and open Agile practices, until it become the norm and new habits were established. It is hard to imagine, now, any other way of working!

Finally, a common misconception was that the

Agile principle of transparency would conflict with the confidential nature of internal audits. However, the adherence of the key Agile principles of trust and discretion within the team, managed this potential issue.

The outcomes:

Overall, the transition to Agile has transformed the way that Internal Audit operates, and made delivery of audit work more transparent and efficient. It has also made what can be traditionally a heavily, structured process, more fun – encouraging open communication and personal interaction.

There has also been a change in the way that Internal Audit managers operate. Managers have shifted to more of a coaching role for the team – emphasising the shared goal of delivering value, and trusting the auditees to self-organise, to deliver the required outcomes.

People outside the Audit team (with perhaps a misperception about the nature of the Audit business) have been surprised, and delighted, about Audit's adoption of Agile. It has also made Auditing Agile projects much more collaborative, transparent and effective. By speaking the same language as the Agile projects, the Internal Audit team is better able to assess the effectiveness of Agile practices in the projects they audit. Finally, it has also allowed more flexibility when it comes to scheduling and responding to changes.

- Adam Spencer, Executive Manager, Suncorp

4: Work, the Agile Way

- Phil Wang, Executive Audit Manager, Suncorp

Kanbans

🗨 'Simplicity, carried to the extreme, becomes elegance.'

Jon Franklin, 1994

Agile processes are designed to promote a sustainable workload, where your Teams, management, and Customers, are able to maintain a constant pace indefinitely. Teams have the authority to design, plan, and estimate, each Iteration, as well as the responsibility and accountability for delivery. This level of ownership for work, combined with integrated Customer engagement, significantly improves workload management, which in turn reduces overtime and stress. However, for this to be efficient, there needs to be a simple mechanism to manage, and level out, workflow within each Team. This is where Kanban comes in. The Kanban development method, as formulated by David Anderson[2], is a Just-In-Time scheduling and workflow framework, to track Requirements and Tasks through their lifecycle.

A Kanban Board is a useful visualisation and control mechanism for both Continuous and Incremental Delivery. Starting at the Backlog, and finishing at Done, each Team will define the intervening states and workflows that make up the lifecycle of their Tasks (the Kanban), which can be as simple, or complex, as required. Teams working on

---

2 *Kanban: Successful Evolutionary Change for Your Technology Business*, Anderson, (2010).

several different types of Tasks may have multiple Kanban Boards, visualising the different states and workflows for each type. When there is available capacity in a state, it will 'pull' any 'Ready' Tasks from the preceding state, thus moving Tasks through the workflow.

 Kanban Board: A tool to visualise and control the workflow of Tasks and Requirements.

Each Team should go through different iterations of their Kanban Board, as their workflow and work processes improve and evolve. It is not unusual for a productive Team, one that has embraced continuous process improvement, to go through several Kanban Board designs a year. A Team that does not change their Kanban Board, is probably only using it to track work, not as a method for improvement.

The visualisation component, or Cards, of a Kanban, helps identify the state of each Task, when a Task is Ready, where there is spare capacity, and if there are any bottlenecks or impediments.

Tasks or Requirements that have identified defects, need rework, or have upstream or downstream dependencies external to the Team that are preventing progress, are marked as 'blocked', but do not change state. By leaving the Task in the current state, the Team can see where the blockage is, and identify where the process should resume once it is resolved. Similarly, by making all blocked Tasks and Requirements visible on the Kanban Board, Customers and management are aware of the issues, and this simplifies any escalation and resolution processes.

Blocked (Kanban): Tasks that have upstream or downstream dependencies external to the Team that are preventing progress.

 The definition of 'Ready' is context specific, and you need to define it explicitly for each state.

The simplest workflow has four states:

1 *Backlog:* Tasks or Requirements that are Ready for work to start. Based on the logical sequencing of Tasks and agreed order, the Team Members select the next Task to work on, and promote this Card to the Active state.

2 *Active:* Tasks or Requirements that are actively being worked on, as defined by the Task or Requirement description. Once the Team Member has completed and shared the Task or Requirement, they promote this Card to the Testing Ready state.

3 *Testing:* Tasks or Requirements that are functionally complete, and undergoing formal validation in order to verify successful completion. Once all Quality Control Tests are Complete, the Task or Requirement is considered Done.

4 *Done:* Tasks or Requirements that are Complete. Different Teams, projects and organisations may have different definitions of Done.

The Assignee for a Task usually changes at each of these steps, though not always. It is important to understand that each column on the Kanban Board represents a state within the development workflow, not a handoff between Team Members. Team Members will proactively interact with their colleagues, and any internal parties, as required, to progress the assigned Task to completion, including any quality control and review.

It is easier to select ordered tasks with a due date.

For both Continuous and Incremental Delivery, the Backlog column is the full Requirements Backlog, and as such, is permanent, but continuously changing as the Team completes Requirements, and the Customer modifies the Backlog. However, for Incremental Delivery, the second state of the Kanban Board, after the Backlog column, is a visualisation of the Iteration Backlog (sometimes known as the input queue), and as such, each new Iteration should clear and replenish it.

Each Task and state should be visible to your Teams, Customer, and Customer Representative; commonly achieved through a physical Kanban Board, or integrated virtual dashboard. Each Kanban Card describes a single Task or Requirement, as well as its estimate, and who is currently working on It. Keep cards simple, with additional information stored elsewhere (usually the workload management system). Divide the Kanban Board into multiple, labelled columns, each representing a single state. Then further divide each column in half, the first half being 'In Progress' and the second half being 'Ready'.

Ready (Kanban): A sub-state within Kanban, for Tasks that are waiting to move to the next state.

In Progress (Kanban): A sub-state within Kanban, for Tasks that are currently being worked on by any member of the Team.

Some versions of Kanban also provide a single 'Expedite' track, at the top of the board, for urgent Requirements and Tasks. There can only ever be one Card at a time in this track, and it has the highest priority, above all other Cards. If possible, Team Members should finish their current Cards before moving onto the Expedited Card. Figure 20 shows a simple version of this flow.

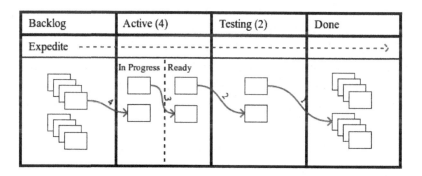

Figure 20: Kanban Board

Except for the Backlog and Done states, the number of Cards allowed at any single time, in each state, is restricted. Called the Work In Progress (WIP) Limit, it includes both the 'In Progress' and 'Ready' Cards in any state, and matches the Team's work capacity. In general, smaller WIP Limits reduce lead times, help uncover problems in the workflow, and drive continuous improvement (Kaizen), whilst higher WIP Limits help to absorb variation and exploit opportunities. Teams using Pair Work will have lower WIP Limits, as there is less simultaneous work in progress. By experimenting with various WIP Limits, you can identify, and resolve, process bottlenecks, adjust the impact of lead time, and create a predictable and efficient workflow. As a rule, your WIP Limit is too low if you hit bottlenecks every week, and too high if blockers don't cause an issue.

When deciding to vary the WIP Limit of a column, Kanban uses the five focusing steps from the Theory of Constraints[3] as the incremental process improvement model. These are:

1 **Identify the system's constraints**: A bottleneck is an extreme example of a constraint. The slowest part of any process, no matter how smoothly it is working, will limit the throughput of the rest of the process.

2 **Decide how to exploit the system's constraints**: Keep the constrained state focused and busy at all times, by focusing on value adding work, removing impediments, and providing high-quality tools and materials.

3 **Subordinate everything else to the above decision**: All other states should not produce more than the constraint can process. This means that, by definition, they have available capacity that can support the constrained state to focus on its core responsibilities.

4 **Elevate the system's constraints**: Once the constrained state has been fully exploited, the Team, or organisation, needs to invest in additional capability, in order to increase its overall capacity.

5 **If, in a previous step, the constraint was broken (e.g. it is no longer a constraint), go back to step one**: At this point, the overall system throughput will have increased, and the system constraint will move to a new point. This encourages continuous improvement (Kaizen) within each Team's processes.

---

3 *The Goal: A Process of Ongoing Improvement*, Goldratt and Cox (1986).

4: Work, the Agile Way

One of the key benefits of creating Cross-Functional Teams, is that is becomes easier to subordinate to, and elevate, a constraint (steps three and four), after identifying a bottleneck. Because the WIP Limit acts as a control mechanism within the system, Team Members are forced to collaborate and change role (e.g. from Working to Testing), rather than continue completing work faster than the constraining state can process it. The Kanban Board provides real time, and clear feedback, on bottlenecks. There is a bottleneck that needs to be resolved when a state is at capacity, and the following state is starved of Cards, or all the Cards in the preceding state are 'Ready' to move on. This visualisation and control of workflow also acts as direct stimuli for continuous and incremental improvement to the Kanban framework, and your overall Agile Business Management process.

Let me finish this section by giving you Toyota's six rules for Kanban[4,5].

1 Do not send defective products to the subsequent process.

2 The subsequent process comes to withdraw only what is needed.

3 Produce only the exact quantity withdrawn by the subsequent process.

4 Equalise, or level, the production.

5 Kanban is a means to fine tuning.

6 Stabilise and rationalise the process.

---

4 *Kanban Just-in Time at Toyota: Management Begins at the* Workplace, Lu and Nōritsu Kyōkai (1986).

5 *Toyota Production System: Beyond Large-Scale Production*, Ohno (1988).

Case study: Exilesoft – Do you dare to ask your HR manager to practise Kanban?

Exilesoft: A mid-sized offshore software development company based in Sri Lanka, specialising in system design, application development, system integration, and business automation.

In 2008, in order to overcome specific offshore challenges, and to improve its quality and productivity, Exilesoft undertook an Agile transformation programme within its project office and delivery teams. While this was highly successful, the rapid change from traditional project culture to Agile culture, as well as the speedy growth of the project organisation, supporting functions such as HR and operations, were unable to meet the demands of the delivery teams. In response, HR department processes became stricter, in order to cope with the situation and continue to deliver results. Yet these attempts often resulted in delays, and a lack of quality in every aspect of their work, from deliverables to services. Given the success of the Agile transformation programme within the delivery teams, senior members of the company believed that using the same Agile concepts within the HR department, would also deliver positive results.

The problems:

After a few rounds of discussions, and careful analysis by engineering staff, project and HR management, greater clarity was obtained about key impediments. These included:

- Inefficient recruitment processes when recruiting software engineers for project requirements.

- Poorly targeted recruitment advertising campaigns that were not attracting senior engineers with the required skills and experience from the market.

- Handling of staff attendance and leave processes was out of sync with the day-to-day needs of the delivery teams.

- HR products and services were not occurring on a timely basis; extending these timelines created chaos in the delivery teams.

- Large and time consuming tasks, such as employee handbook creation, were often delivered late, and over several months.

- Incompatible employee evaluation processes with the delivery team culture.

The causes:

Most of the root causes of these problems related to the history that traditional offshore development processes, involving the remote Customer and the development teams, had faced before adapting to Agile practices.

- The HR department was isolated from the delivery teams.

- HR, and the delivery teams, had different understandings of what Agile meant.

- Most requests, such as recruitment needs, were

sent to the HR department over e-mail, causing a lack of appreciation for the specific needs of the individual.

• Too much to do.

The solution:

To improve productivity, and resolve many of the problems above, the HR department agreed to try out a selected Agile method for their day-to-day operations. The initial idea was to implement Scrum processes, however, this was quickly discarded, as there were many foreseen difficulties. Primarily, the nature of HR deliverables meant a greater amount of ad hoc requests outside the Iteration cycle, many of which required immediate delivery outside the scheduled release (Iteration) cycle.

It was decided that Kanban would be a better fit for the HR department over the Scrum processes practised by Exilesoft's delivery teams. Kanban supported daily planning, continuous delivery, visible progress (through the Kanban Board), optional estimation, and cycle time monitoring (e.g. monitoring the time taken for a new employee to sign in with Exilesoft, from the time the request for the vacancy was raised). In addition, the concept of limiting Work In Process (WIP) prevented the HR department from committing to work on various tasks that would exceed their capacity. Instead, selecting the right priority, focusing on them, and delivering them faster, could deliver better results.

Lastly, by removing the separation between the HR department and the delivery teams, the expectation was to reduce any dependencies that may create latency. Further, this would avoid the 'over the wall' approach, and was expected to create better understanding, respect, and communication between people working in both the entities.

The implementation:

The HR team was given sufficient training to convert from traditional management thinking to Agile leadership and team play thinking. To manage the incoming requirements for the HR department, it was agreed to use the same backlog format as the delivery teams. For example

Table 5: Example HR Requirements

ID	As a/an/the	I need	So that
1	CEO of the company	All the employees to be aware of the company administration policies	There will be lesser day-to-day issues to be handled with regard to disciplinary issues
2	Team lead	To have an event organised for the team, to celebrate the upcoming final release of the project	We can recognise the team effort

3	Staff	To produce a letter to the Australian Migration office before end of November	I can prove my work experience needed for the PR application
4	Project director	Five new recruits in Java tech lead calibre by 1st week of December 2009	We can initiate the new automated warehouse product development

To visualise progress, the HR manager's office wall was originally used as the task board. The stories were pasted in the stack column, and the highest priority stories were broken into tasks, and pasted in the 'To do' column. Identically coloured sticky notes were used to identify the tasks falling under one User Story.

Figure 21: Exilesoft – Example Card

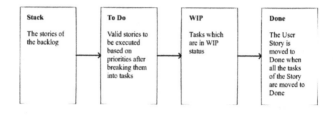

Figure 22: Exilesoft – Kanban Board

Finally, the HR team conducted daily meetings in front of the Kanban Board at 9.30 am Sri Lankan time; limited to 20 minutes. When there were other teams involved for specific tasks, those teams also participated in the same meeting, in order to update the HR team about their progress and dependencies.

The challenges:

The key challenges were as follows:

- **Transparent tasks on the Kanban Board.** Some tasks reflected sensitive information to the staff. To avoid such display of tasks on the HR manager's office wall, it was decided to have a web-based Kanban tool.

- **Minor ad hoc tasks.** There were many smaller tasks flowing to the HR department daily. A guideline had to be agreed by the team members about the size of the tasks taken in to the Kanban Board.

- **Dealing with daily routine tasks.** Those tasks were handled outside the Kanban Board. The members decided on a six-hour Kanban day, instead of an eight-hour day, in order to leave room for such work.

- **Difference of team culture to the delivery teams which requires ongoing analysis.**

The outcomes:

The above implementation delivered visible, and positive, results after six months. The HR department, and the delivery teams, started to work more closely, with a better understanding of each other's capacity, priorities, and the expected level of quality. This created a more solution-focused culture at Exilesoft, instead of different entities trying to pass the work, and blame each other. Some of the key visibilities:

- The HR department is much more productive

than before.

- Communication and delegation among the HR staff has greatly improved.

- Most discussions with the delivery teams are now handled via casual discussions, instead of issuing formal letters, and calling for formal meetings.

- The annual review process has changed to more frequent reviews, which are expected to reinforce, and energise, the culture in a positive manner.

- The company's Agile maturity is used in the recruitment process to attract better candidates who want to work in a different culture, against the typical offshore software factory culture.

- The HR department empowers more team activities in the organisation, such as arts competitions, and games among the teams.

- The HR department has won more recognition from the project organisation, due to their genuine effort to facilitate the performance of the project organisation.

Today, Exilesoft has overcome most of the key challenges of such Agile transition, by standardising the same concepts across other entities, such as the HR department. This transformation has resulted in productivity improvements, and better, self-motivated teams across the organisation.

- Thushara Wijewardena, Chief Project Officer, Exilesoft

Quality control

Q 'Failure is simply the opportunity to begin again, this time more intelligently. There is no disgrace in honest failure; there is disgrace in fearing to fail.'

Henry Ford, 1922

Quality control, whether formal and systematic, or informal and ad hoc, is the responsibility of every individual, Team, and Department, and should cover each stage of the work lifecycle. In project management, there is a saying, 'Fast, Good, or Cheap; pick two', and while it may sometimes be true, under an Agile Business Management approach, quality controls are embedded within the work lifecycle, thus taking it out of the equation.

Dedicated testers embedded within each Team undertake quality control, while still ensuring a separation between the doers and testers. Regardless of whether your Team uses Incremental or Continuous Delivery, one tester per Team (between five-nine people) should be able run complete Quality Control Tests at roughly the same rate as Requirements are completed. High-risk or high-complexity Requirements may require additional testers per Team (or smaller Teams); play with the Team numbers until you reach that perfect point where everyone is busy, but no one is being a bottleneck. A Kanban Board is a simple way of visualising bottlenecks, as per Figure 23.

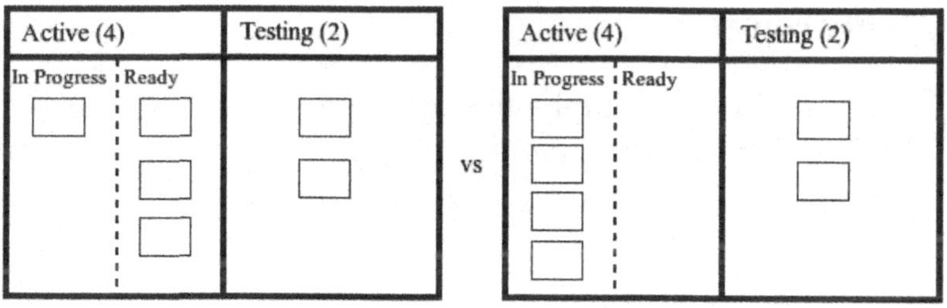

Figure 23: Bottlenecked vs. clear Kanban Boards

In smaller organisations, and Teams without formal quality control processes, doers could take on testing responsibilities, as long as they do not test their own work.

Embedding quality control within your Teams, also simplifies internal approval and sign-off processes. Assuming a level of trust, and let's face it, if you don't trust your testers, you have bigger problems than quality control, senior executives should only need to undertake cursory examinations prior to approving the Deliverables for Release. This will improve overall efficiency, and reduce any tendency towards micromanagement. As an Agile Manager, you may not think the work is perfect, but as long as it fulfils the Customers' Requirements, and meets all agreed quality standards, there should be no reason for you to send it back for re-work.

Remember Agile principle #1: Our highest priority is to satisfy the customer, through early and continuous delivery of valuable software [Requirements].

The responsibilities of the dedicated testers are to:

- Validate Deliverables against Customer Requirements.

- Ensure that Deliverables quality meets Customer expectations.

- Check that the Deliverables follows appropriate corporate standards (such as using correct document templates).

- Undertake low-level, or fine-grained, analysis of Deliverables, such as checking spelling and grammar, validating budget line items, or materials workmanship.

- Check that the new Deliverables integrate with existing Deliverables, or existing products (integration testing).

- Validate that any replacement Deliverables continue to meet the same standards as the previous version (regression testing).

- Provide ongoing testing throughout each stage of work.

- Validate that all outputs comply with relevant legislation, or industry standards.

- If relevant, or required, check that the outputs are usable by all potential consumers, including disabled people.

- If relevant, check that different versions of the same product are functionally identical (e.g. in different languages).

As a final step to ensure high-quality outcomes for the Customer, Agile Business Management draws on the 'Test-Driven Development' software engineering Agile method. As described earlier, Test-Driven Development requires that software developers create several tests, generally fully automated, before building a new feature. If, after the Requirement is complete, the new tests pass, then the software is displaying correct behaviour.

The core concept of writing Quality Control Tests before beginning work on any Requirement applies, just as well, to any Requirement. Let's call this 'Test-Driven Work' (TDW), the art of Test First, Test Often. How should HR confirm they recruited the right person for the role? What validation will Finance and Accounting undertake to ensure that the annual report is correct? How will Media and Communications ensure that the new advertising campaign was successful? And, of course, how will your Delivery Teams verify that the product meets your Customer's expectations?

 Test-Driven Work: The act of writing Quality Control Tests prior to beginning any work, rather than after.

 Automated Quality Control Test: A Quality Control Test that can be regularly run without human interaction.

There are six main steps to Test-Driven Work, for each new Task or Requirement.

1 Create a Quality Control Test in conjunction with the Customer (and add the tests to the test catalogue).

2 Validate the Quality Control Test is correct.

3 Do the work (fulfil the Requirement).

4 Run all related tests from the test catalogue, not just the new test.

5 Clean up the work, to ensure it meets corporate standards, and can be easily integrated with related Requirements.

6 Repeat.

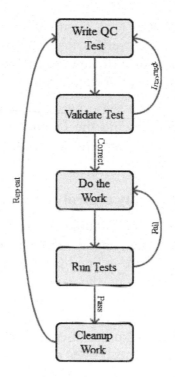

Figure 24: Test-Driven Work flowchart

The first point is often overlooked; your Team and Customers, in collaboration, should create Quality Control Tests. By working together and pre-defining the tests, the Team can easily measure progress towards meeting the Customers' agreed expectations, e.g. 15 out of 50 Story Points have passed quality control. The Customer can then make informed decisions about the Deliverable. This also means that the Team can honestly claim a Requirement is Done, even before the final Customer sign off. Your Customer can change their mind about the Requirement later, but the Team should be working efficiently, and accurately, within their current understanding.

By running all related tests from the test catalogue (Point 4), your Team can verify that the newly completed Requirement has not affected negatively on previously completed, and accepted, Requirements.

A little bit of common sense needs to be applied here; the more variables influencing the Quality Control Tests will reduce the accuracy of the check, and the effectiveness of the Requirement itself.

 Example quality control scenarios

Media and Communications have created an advertising campaign to test the market for a new product. The pre-defined Quality Control Test (10% increased sales of the new product) demonstrates that the advertising campaign was a success. However, related Quality Control Tests may show that the campaign has alienated existing consumers, resulting in reduced sales of other products.

 Example quality control scenarios

Our advertising campaign failed to meet the 10% increased sales Quality Control Test. This does not necessarily mean that the advertising campaign was of poor quality. It may have been because:

- The product itself is deficient
- The economy went into depression
- The new iPhone was released, so no one has any money.

If a completed Requirement fails a Quality Control Test once or twice, it will generally be the work at fault. However, if it consistently fails the test, you need to start looking beyond the work, for other factors that may be affecting it.

For further detail, there are many excellent books written on the subject of quality control, quality assurance and Test-Driven Development[6,7,8].

The Daily Stand-up and Agile meetings

'There is nothing so useless as doing efficiently that which should not be done at all.'

Peter Drucker, 2003

The Daily Stand-up is a short Team meeting that provides a consistent focus on progress, and a forum for your Teams to discuss issues. The Daily Stand-up is not a status report; it is an informative, and interactive, discussion, that informs the Team's understanding of what is happening, by whom, and its progress. This is the key inspection and transparency mechanism within the Team.

 Daily Stand-up: A daily, 15 minute, Team meeting, to discuss progress, plans and issues.

This meeting consists of the Customer (or Customer Representative), Team Facilitator, and the Team, and is restricted to 15 minutes. Non-Team Members are welcome to watch the Daily Stand-up, though, they are restricted

6 *Test-Driven Development by Example*, Beck (2002).

7 *Refactoring: Improving the Design of Existing Code*, Fowler and Beck (1999).

8 *The Management and Control of Quality*, Evans and Lindsay (2008).

from participating during the 15 minutes, and the Team Facilitator is responsible for enforcing this.

All participants should answer the following three questions:

1 What did you achieve yesterday (or since the last Stand-up)?
2 What will you achieve today (or before the next Stand-up)?
3 What impediments may prevent you from achieving your goal?

The Daily Stand-up is run, primarily, for the benefit of the Team, and so each Team, not management, is responsible for running their own Daily Stand-up. It is the responsibility of the Team Facilitator to ensure the Daily Stand-up runs smoothly, is restricted to 15 minutes, and record any impediments identified by the Team. Strong facilitation by the Team Facilitator is the key to a good Daily Stand-up, rather than any set agenda. The Team Facilitator watches, and directs, the flow of the conversation, to cover all topics, whilst enforcing the strict time limit. Stand-ups that exceed the allocated time can significantly affect the time available to deliver Requirements, and participants who are not directly involved in the conversation will quickly lose interest. Schedule follow-on discussions to discuss issues identified during the Stand-up. This means that only those with an interest in the issue stay, and everyone else can return to work, with minimal interruption.

Anyone familiar with Scrum will recognise this as similar to the Daily Scrum.

Departments, or projects, with multiple Teams, should hold a Summary Stand-up, also restricted to 15 minutes, after the initial Stand-up. This gathering should bring together Team Facilitators (or relevant Team Members) from multiple Teams, to answer the same three questions as before, but relating to their Teams.

 Summary Stand-up: A Daily Stand-up consisting of representatives from each of the Teams with a Department or project.

Do not hold meetings, gatherings, or workshops, without a well-defined need. However, if they are required, they should be facilitated, and strictly timeboxed. With a good facilitator tracking time and content, the conversation can flow dynamically, as needed by the participants. Facilitation to this level is very difficult, and needs someone who can manage conflicting needs, maintain neutrality on the issues discussed, remain assertive without being overbearing, and mix in a bit of common sense. Creating, and keeping to, simple agendas, can be useful, to ensure participants are on track and meetings on time, but meetings will still require facilitation.

Effort estimation

> 'There is only one good, knowledge, and one evil, ignorance.'
>
> Socrates, ~3rd Century CE

Estimating Requirements

Without a clear understanding of the effort involved to deliver a Requirement, it is impossible for your Team to accurately plan their work; both at a macro level, defining a final delivery date, or micro level, assigning Requirements into Iterations. Taking a highly successful concept from Agile, you can use Story Points, and Story Point estimation, to provide a mechanism by which Teams can estimate effort. A Story Point is an arbitrary single number intended to represent all of the effort required for the whole Team to complete a single Requirement, and are relative to an initial, simple reference Requirement (or User Story). By selecting the simplest, best understood, Requirement possible, and defining that as one Story Point, the Team can estimate all future Requirements as a multiple of this reference Requirement[9].

 Story Point: An arbitrary number intended to represent all of the effort required for the whole Team to complete a single Requirement, relative to a reference Requirement.

For high-level estimates, Story Points are generally better than time estimates, as they factor in non-time based complexity and uncertainties. As an estimate of complexity, they are not as affected by specific Team performance, and so tend to have less variation. There have also been numerous studies showing that, on average, Teams are better at relative estimation than absolute estimation.

To make a Story Point estimate requires representation of all the skills needed for delivery during the estimation

---

9 *Agile Estimating and Planning*, Cohn (2005).

process. Your Team is ultimately accountable for the estimate, and while management and the Customer can provide input, only the Team understands the effort required. Extending this means that only your Team can make the estimate, not you, other managers, business analysts, or the Customer.

Use Story Points for the high-level estimation of Requirements, and reference the effort involved in the delivery of similar Requirements. As the reference Requirement is Team specific, different Teams will have different definitions of a Story Point. Assuming that a Team is relatively constant, the size of a Story Point for that Team will eventually normalise over time.

Q Your Teams may need to re-baseline the reference Requirement, as the type of Requirements change, or they find too many sub-one Story Point Requirements.

Your Teams will estimate, and re-estimate, Requirements, whenever the Customer modifies the Requirements Backlog. Updated and revised estimates take into account new information, as well as improvements in the estimation process itself.

Estimating tasks

Story Points are an excellent, long-term, average predictor, but lose definition if used for short-term estimation. If your Teams break Requirement into Tasks during the planning phase of Incremental Delivery, then an indication of how many hours effort is required for each Task, is important for good planning.

A Task effort estimate is not the same as duration (e.g. three hours efforts > three hours duration). Converting effort into duration needs to take into account staff overheads, such as breaks, meetings, illness, and assisting other Team Members. To calculate estimated duration, multiple staff overhead to the estimated effort.

 Staff Overhead: Any time used by a staff member during working hours, not in the delivery of Tasks or Requirements. Overhead includes; breaks, meetings, illness, and assisting other Team Members.

 Effort: Only the specific time required to complete a Task or Requirement, excluding any overhead.

The algorithm to calculate staff overhead (per Iteration) is as follows:

Working Hours = (hours per day * days per Iteration * staff) – planned leave

Actual Hours = sum of actual (from last Iteration)

Staff Overhead = Working Hours/Actual Hours

 Example estimate to duration calculation:

Working Hours = (8 * 10 * 5) – 0 = 400

Actual Hours = 300

Staff Overhead = (400/300) = 1.3

Effort Estimate = 5 hours

Duration = 5 * 1.3 = 6.5 hours

Working Hours: The total time a Team Member spends at work (usually between 7.5 and 8 hours per day).

 Actual Hours: The total effort to complete a Task or Requirement, as measured when complete.

Estimation process

Though they use different measures, the estimation process for Requirements (Story Points) and Tasks (Effort) is the same[10].

To simplify the estimation process, and ensure that estimates are realistic, estimates are chosen from the modified Fibonacci series; 1, 2, 3, 5, 8, 13, 20, 40, and 100. There are three benefits to using this sequence:

1 Improved design – it encourages features to be split into a reasonable size.

2 Estimate skill – people are better at estimating small Tasks, so it provides a more realistic range.

3 Meaningful estimates – though the same value, the difference in estimate between 1 and 2 is meaningful, whereas the difference between 20 and 21 is not.

There are four primary methods for estimating Requirements and Tasks:

1 *Expert opinion:* The Team Member with specific understanding, or who is most likely to develop the Task or Requirement, can provide a more accurate estimate of

---

10 *Agile Estimating and Planning*, Cohn (2005).

effort. For example, an accountant can better estimate effort for finance Tasks.

2 *Comparison:* Comparing a Task or Requirement to another, already estimated, Task. For example, 'Hiring four Team Members is about twice the effort of hiring two Team Members'.

3 *Components:* If a Task or Requirement is too large to estimate accurately, break it into small Sub-Tasks. For example, designing a promotion can be broken into traditional media, social media, graphic design, printing, etc.

4 *Historical statistics:* If a Task or Requirement is nearly identical in outcomes, size, and complexity to a previous Task or Requirement, then use the actual effort of the previous, as the estimate of the new. For example, resetting a user's password takes almost the same time, regardless of who it is for, or when it is requested.

Other methods can help improve the estimation process. One of the most popular is Planning Poker. Developed in 2002 by James Grenning[11], Planning Poker is an estimation game, using a special set of cards (based on the modified Fibonacci series above), that promotes collaboration and consensus building during the estimation process. Figure 25 shows a sample of these cards.

---

11 *Planning Poker or How to Avoid Analysis Paralysis while Release Planning,* Grenning (2002).

Figure 25: Sample Planning Poker Cards (Mountain Goat Software)

The Team starts by discussing each Requirement or Task, but without mentioning any estimates, to avoid influencing other Team Members. When ready, each person lays a card face down representing their estimate of the Task, and, when all Team Members are ready, simultaneously turns their cards over. The Team Members who selected the highest and lowest estimates have the opportunity to discuss their reasoning, before the Team plays again. It is the responsibility of the Team Facilitator to build consensus, and facilitate the quick, but open, discussion.

Measuring progress

> 'Let us labour for that larger and larger comprehension of truth, that more and more thorough repudiation of error, which shall make the history of mankind a series of ascending developments.'

4: Work, the Agile Way

Horace Mann, 1867

In order to know what is Done, and to plan future Requirements, each Team must measure their rate of progress. In Agile terms this is called Velocity. Velocity is a measure that determines the capacity, and resulting output from the Team, over time. Put more simply, it is the rate at which your Teams can deliver Requirements, as measured by Story Points. Each Team will have their own Velocity, and as the Team composition and experiences change, so will the Velocity. Teams that use Continuous rather than Incremental Delivery (such as HR), will calculate their Velocity in the same way, Requirements delivered over time. However, rather than use Iterations, these teams would use a fixed reporting period, such as a week. This period would also feed into their Retrospective cycle.

Velocity should be constantly calculated, and recalculated, from previous rates of delivery. However, this assumes, a) that this Team has completed at least one previous Requirement, b) that the new Requirements are of similar composition, and c) the process for estimating the new Requirements is equivalent. If any of these are not true, then the Team should make a guess of their Velocity for planning purposes. Calculate the actual Velocity after the first Iteration is complete.

Example Velocity calculation:

Iteration 1

Requirement 1: 5sp

Requirement 3: 7sp

Total: 12sp

Iteration 2

Requirement 4: 3sp

Requirement 6: 5sp

Requirement 2: 1sp

Requirement 9: 6sp (incomplete)

Total: 9sp + 6sp (incomplete)

Iteration 3

Requirement 9: 6sp

Requirement 10: 6sp

Requirement 10: 5sp (incomplete)

Total: 12sp + 5sp (incomplete)

Velocity = ((5+7) + (3+5+1) + (6+6)) / 3

= (12 + 9 + 12) / 3

= 11sp / Iteration

As each Requirement is completed, tested, and approved, it should be marked 'Done' in the Requirements Backlog. This tells all stakeholders that the Requirement has been finished, that it is ready for the Customer, and can be included in the Velocity calculations. Incomplete Requirements at the end of an Iteration do not count towards the Velocity, as Agile does not make the distinction between 0% complete, 50% complete or 99% complete. However, this is not an issue, as Velocity averages out over multiple Iterations, and factors in minor variations due to partially completed Requirements.

It is not meaningful to talk about Task Velocity. The rate at which a Team Member completes Effort Hours is directly proportional to the staff overhead. For example, based on the previous example 6 hours of work per day = 8/6 = 1.3 = staff overhead.

However, Velocity is only one part of the story. For many Teams (such as Support Teams), it is important to also measure the time a Requirement sits in the Backlog before being actioned, or the time a Requirement sits in each state (e.g. the time taken to move from Active to Testing, and from Testing to Done). The primary measures for this are Lead Time and Cycle Time. Unlike Velocity, Lead Time and Cycle Time do not measure effort, but the elapsed time (or duration). Figure 26 shows the relationship between Cycle Time and Lead Time.

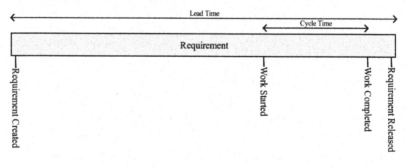

Figure 26: Cycle Time

 Lead Time: The time taken between adding a Requirement to the Requirements Backlog, and Releasing it to the Customer.

Cycle Time: The time taken between starting, and completing, work on a Requirement.

When each Task is Complete, it should also be marked as Done in the Iteration Backlog. It is optional whether Team Members record an 'actual' time spent against each Task. However, by recording the actual effort spent (not including breaks, meetings, etc.), it is possible to validate, and improve, the Task estimation process, and easily calculate staff overhead at the end of the Iteration. However, this can put additional pressure on Teams, and, depending on how the information is used, may not result in improved outcomes.

There can be significant pushback against getting Team Members to record actual time, mostly due to fear of punishment, or performance management. It is important for the Team to understand that the goal of measurement is to empower and improve the Team, not micromanage them. It doesn't matter if their overhead is 1.3 (6 hours' work per day) or 10.3 (45 mins work per day), as long as your Teams are being utilised appropriately, and, as a manager, you understand why their overheads are high.

Visualising progress

Q 'However beautiful the strategy, you should occasionally look at the results.'

Winston Churchill, anecdotal

Numbers alone don't provide enough useful information to manage your Teams. Using Burndown Charts, Cumulative Flow Diagrams, and Cycle Time Run Charts, you can represent, and visualise, the scope of work, planned delivery, and actual delivery of Tasks and Requirements. To ensure full transparency between your Teams and Customers, these Charts should be available to everyone even remotely involved with the Team.

 Burndown Chart: A visualisation of the total effort, and effort remaining, against time.

 Cumulative Flow Diagram: A visualisation of the elapsed time, and number of Tasks or Requirements remaining in each state, against time.

 Cycle Time Run Chart: A visualisation of the Cycle Time (or Lead Time), compared with the average Cycle Time and bounded by the expected tolerances.

Burndown Charts

Your Customer will mostly be interested in the Release Burndown Chart, which shows the progress of the Team in delivering Requirements (by Story Points) over time. The Team can use the Iteration (Task) Burndown Chart to view progress against the Iteration, improve future estimates, and identify problem trends early.

A Burndown Chart, as shown in Figure 27, graphs the total effort estimated, and estimated effort remaining against time, either the length of an Iteration, or a reportable period. The Y-Axis is the sum of all effort within the Iteration Backlog, and the X-Axis is the number of working days in the Iteration. The diagonal line between the top left and bottom right will visualise your expected Velocity (i.e. you should be able to finish all Tasks in the Backlog within a single Iteration). To visualise and monitor progress, plot the sum of the remaining effort each day.

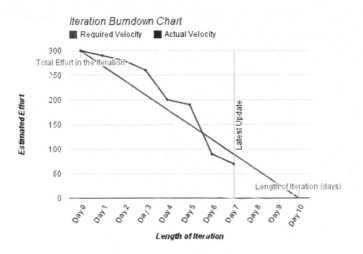

Figure 27: Example Burndown Chart

💡 Remember Agile principle #7: Working software [completed Requirements] is the primary measure of progress.

Similar to the Iteration Burndown Chart, the Release Burnup Chart (Figure 28) visualises the total effort estimated, and estimated effort remaining in the Requirements Backlog, against the expected release delivery dates (usually measured in Iterations). Like the Iteration Burndown Chart, the Y-Axis of the Release Burnup Chart is the sum of all effort within the Requirements Backlog (measured in Story Points), and the X-Axis is the number of Iterations, or weeks, until final

Release date, or next major milestone. To chart your Customer's changing Requirements, plot a line showing the sum of all Requirements per Iteration. Finally, the Required Velocity and Actual Velocity lines visualise progress towards completing the Requirements Backlog.

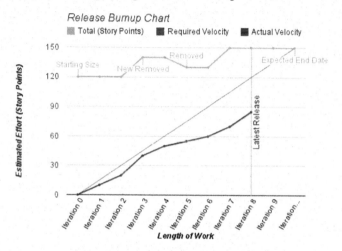

Figure 28: Example Burnup Chart

Burndown Charts can help identify problem areas and future risks. These include:

- **Discovery**
  - *Identified by:* A sharp rise on the first day of the Iteration.

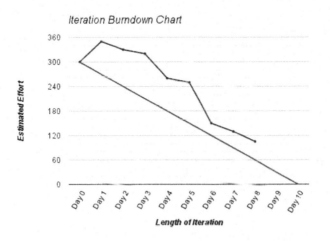

Figure 29: Problem Burndown (Discovery)

- *Identified Issue:* Immediately after the Iteration begins, issues have been identified, or estimates refined.
- *Resolution:* Watch the progress carefully, and if necessary, review the Tasks in the Iteration.

- **Scope creep**
  - *Identified by:* Tracking close to the expected Velocity, followed by a sharp rise mid-way through the Iteration.

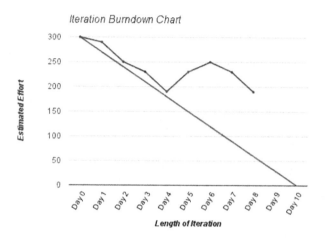

Figure 30: Problem Burndown (Scope creep)

  - *Identified issue:* This is caused by Tasks being added mid-Iteration, which leads to poor delivery rates, useless estimates, and wasted effort.
  - *Resolution:* Identify who is adding Tasks, and stop this behaviour. In addition, if the new Tasks are truly more important, then the current Iteration should be stopped, and a new Iteration planned.

- **Plateau**
  o *Identified by:* Tracking well, followed by no visible progress for several days.

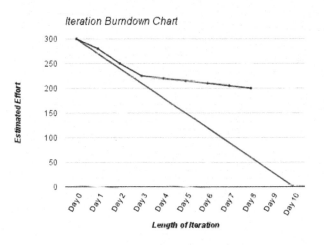

Figure 31: Problem Burndown (Plateau)

  o *Identified issue:* Progress has frozen, usually due to Requirements being more difficult than estimated, or unexpected staffing issues.
  o *Resolution:* Review the Tasks in the Iteration.

- **Too many features**
  - o *Identified by:* A steady burndown of work, but a growing distance between actual, and expected, Velocity.

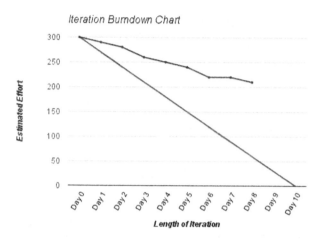

Figure 32: Problem Burndown (Too many features)

- o *Identified issue:* Progress is progressing much slower than expected, generally caused by overloaded staff, or poor estimation.
- o *Resolution:* Review the estimation process, and remove Tasks from the Iteration.

- **Stories are too large**
  - o *Identified by:* Starting out looking like Plateau, followed by a sharp drop.

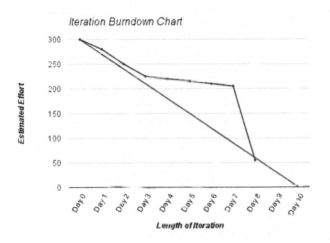

Figure 33: Problem Burndown (Stories are too large)

- o *Identified issue:* Individual Tasks are too large, and thus difficult to track.
- o *Resolution:* Keep each Task under one day of effort.

- **Nothing wrong**
  - o Tracking close to the expected Velocity

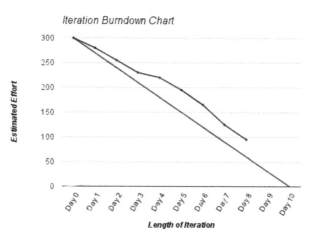

Figure 34: Normal Burndown

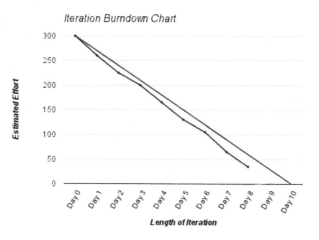

Figure 35: Normal Burndown

Cumulative Flow Diagrams

Like the Burndown Chart, a Cumulative Flow Diagram (CFD) visualises the flow of work over time, as shown in Figure 36. However, where the Burndown Chart visualises delivery against estimates, which is useful in verifying that work is on track, the CFD visualises delivery against elapsed time, which is useful in verifying that the delivery of work is efficient.

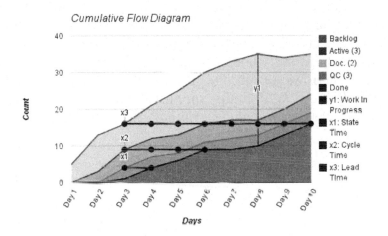

Figure 36: Example Cumulative Flow Diagram

The CFD tracks each state in your workflow separately, from when a card (or Task) enters that state, to the time the card enters the subsequent state. The vertical distance (y1) in each charted line shows the number of Tasks currently in progress. This distance should never be greater than the WIP limit for the state. The horizontal distance (x1) shows the time taken for a Task to progress to the next state. The horizontal distance (x2) shows the Average Cycle Time, the time taken from when a Card leaves the Backlog state, until is it Done. The final horizontal distance (x3) shows the Average Lead Time, the time taken from when the Card enters the Backlog, until it is Done. Like the Burndown Chart, this will also help predict when all the work is Done.

Cumulative Flow Diagrams can also help estimate the time required (not the Effort) to deliver new Tasks or Requirements, but only if they are all of equivalent size and complexity.

Each line on the Cumulative Flow Diagram should appear smooth; any flat vertical or horizontal generally indicates impediments, or an uneven flow of work. You can quickly, and easily, identify bottlenecks, when the area between two bands narrows or, in the worst case, reduces to zero. Keeping low WIP limits simplifies the identification of bottlenecks, when analysing Cumulative Flow Diagrams.

- **Bottleneck**
  - o *Identified by:* A band reducing to zero.

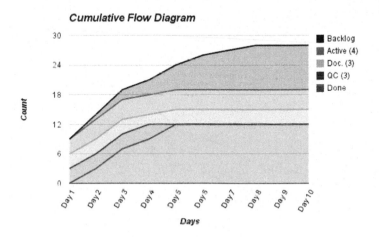

Figure 37: Problem CFD (Starved state)

- o *Identified issue:* The Documentation state is a bottleneck in the process, and has starved the Quality Control state of any work.
- o *Resolution:* Improve the delivery through the bottlenecked state by exploiting, subordinating, and elevating the constraint (*see section: Kanbans*).

- **Poor flow**
  - o *Identified by:* Jagged, widening, and narrowing bands, between two or more states.

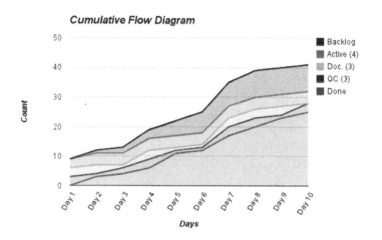

Figure 38: Problem CFD (Poor flow)

- o *Identified issue:* Caused when there is not a smooth flow of work through the system. States that jump to the maximum WIP, and back down again, can also be indicative of bottlenecks, or other impediments, throughout the work processes.
- o *Resolution:* Identify the cause of the impediments of bottlenecks, and remove them, to improve the flow of work.

- **No, or large, WIP Limit**
  o *Identified by:* A large distance between each band, causing a false sense of smoothness.

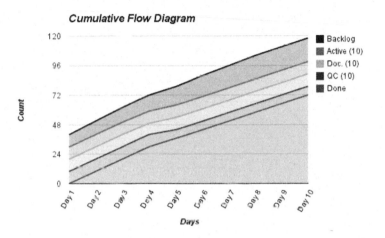

Figure 39: Problem CFD (Large WIP)

  o *Identified issue:* This example actually shows the same variation as the 'Bottleneck' example above. However, as the WIP Limit is very large, it is difficult to identify any fluctuations in the chart.
  o *Resolution:* Reduce the WIP Limit to an appropriate number.

- **Long lead time**
  - o *Identified by:* A very slow, and shallow, rise in all states.

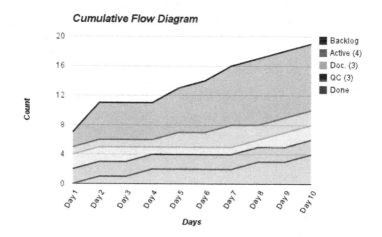

Figure 40: Problem CFD (Long lead time)

- o *Identified issue:* There is a long lead time (and cycle time) between raising a Requirement, and it being Delivered to the Customer.
- o *Resolution:* Reduce the WIP Limit, or reduce the size of the Requirements, to improve the speed of the workflow.

- **Plateau**
  o *Identified by:* Tracking well, followed by no visible progress for several days.

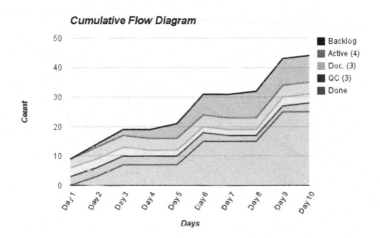

Figure 41: Problem CFD (Plateau)

o *Identified issue.* The flow of work has stopped (or dramatically slowed), usually caused by critical production issues, large-scale staff absences (e.g. Christmas holidays), or waiting for Customer sign off.

o *Resolution:* Identify what is causing the halt of workflow, and (if appropriate) resolve the underlying issue.

- **Nothing wrong**
  - o Tracking well in terms of consistent rise, and no major widening or narrowing of bands.

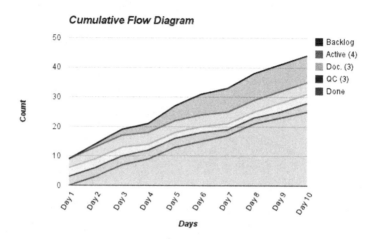

Figure 42: Normal CFD

Cycle Time Run Charts

Teams that measure Cycle Time and Lead Time can visualise these metrics using Cycle Time Run Charts (sometimes known as statistical process control charts). By looking for trends, cycles and outliers, Cycle Time Run Charts will help you to identify both normal, and uncontrolled, variations in process flow. Noting, of course, that all processes will show some variation.

As described in **Error! Not a valid result for table.**, it is important to understand which variations are normal (common causes), and which variations are out of control (special causes).

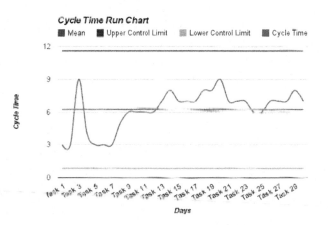

Figure 43: Example Run Chart

Run Charts plot the Cycle (or Lead) Time of each Requirement, against the long-term average, known as the centre line. From a continuous improvement perspective, you should aim to improve your work processes, so the centre line (and thus your average Cycle Time) meets your Customer's needs.

If you know the expected variance within your process (usually ± three standard deviations), you can plot the Upper Control Limit (UCL) and Lower Control Limit (LCL). These limits are the primary mechanism to identify special cause events. This means you should investigate any Cycle Times outside these limits, as they can indicate a process out of control.

 Control Limit: The bounds of expected variance within the Team's processes. Processes that exceed these control limits can be said to be uncontrolled.

It is simple to calculate Cycle Time Run Charts when all Customer Requirements are of approximately equal size and effort. However, they can still be effective for Requirements of varying sizes, but will have higher Control Limits, and need a larger dataset to calculate a meaningful average.

 Teams that work on multiple types of Requirements may have multiple Run Charts, one for each type. For example, HR may have a recruitment Run Chart and a performance management Run Chart.

- **Process trend**
  - o *Identified by:* A run of points that are continuously increasing or decreasing.

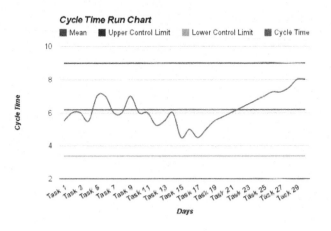

Figure 44: Problem Run Chart (Process trend)

- o *Identified issue:* There is a progressive trend in the Cycle Time, implying that something is gradually shifting over time.
- o *Resolution:* If the trend is in the right direction (usually down), it may be part of ongoing process improvement, and your Team should sustain the change. Otherwise, your Team needs to determine the cause of the variation, and resolve it.

- **Process shift**
  - o *Identified by:* A run of points on a single side of the centre line.

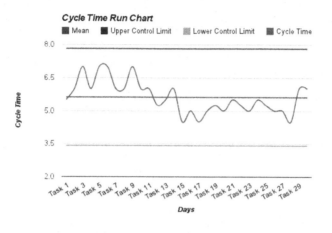

Figure 45: Problem Run Chart (Process shift)

- o *Identified issue:* There is a sustained shift in Cycle Time, and may have reached a new equilibrium.
- o *Resolution:* If the shift is in the right direction (usually down), it may be part of ongoing process improvement, and your Team should sustain the change. Otherwise, your Team needs to determine the cause of the variation, and resolve it.

Extreme process variation

o *Identified by:* Points above the UCL, or below the LCL.

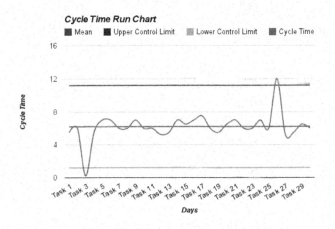

Figure 46: Problem Run Chart (Extreme process variation)

o *Identified issue:* Extreme variation (special causes) in the Team's process that may indicate a process out of control.

o *Resolution:* Identify the cause of the outliers, and if systemic, resolve the underlying issues.

- **Nothing wrong**
  - o No major variations in process flow.

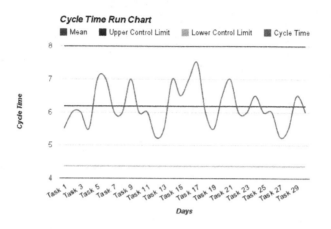

Figure 47: Normal Run Chart

CHAPTER 5: THE AGILE BUDGET

Funding models

Q 'Costs do not exist to be calculated. Costs exist to be reduced.'

Taiichi Ohno, 1988

Aim of this chapter: To define the associated financial models and processes that support your Agile organisation. We will look at Agile budgeting and delegation options, as well as how to manage budgets, quotes and costings, alongside changing Customer Requirements.

Most organisations plan funding by financial year, and allocate it to Departments for business-as-usual activities, or temporary projects for a specific outcome. This, in turn, is generally broken into capital, and operational, expenditure. However, a lot can happen in a year. Teams with long-term fixed budgets may not be in a position to take advantage of new opportunities, or adapt to meet changing Customer Requirements.

Where possible, Agile organisations should adopt the following three major changes to funding models to ensure Teams, Departments, and projects, remain adaptable.

1 **Monthly or quarterly budgets:** By reducing the duration of each budget, organisations can tailor funding to meet the current needs of a Team, or Department. As most budget proposals will be identical, or nearly identical, to previous months, there is negligible

overhead in managing multiple, short, budgets. Teams and Departments are encouraged (and in some cases incentivised) to be innovative with their existing budgets, and, where possible, reduce outgoing expenditure.

 Example budget change request

The Sales and Marketing Team (the Customer) approach the Communications Team (the Team) to deliver a new, social media advertising campaign, to take advantage of a new opportunity. The Communications Team does not have the skills for this, and so puts forward a new budget proposal that includes a social media communications strategist. The Finance Team, in charge of the budgets, examine the proposal, and approves it based on the expected benefits, allowing the Communications Team to recruit within two weeks.

2 **Team level contingency:** As part of their monthly budget, allocate each Team a contingency budget (usually ~20%) to spend at their discretion, either in the delivery of Customer Requirements, or as a mechanism to innovate change within the organisation. Unused contingency should carry over, to encourage sensible spending, rather than the traditional 'use it or lose it' approach.

 Example uses of contingency:

- The R&D Team use their contingency budget to replace a defective stress-test machine (the replacement cost was low enough that they did not need to increase their budget proposal).

- The ICT Support Team uses their contingency to subscribe to an IT journal (after checking that no one else had already subscribed).

- The HR Team, having recently had a large turnover in staff, use their contingency on team-building exercises.

- A Delivery Team uses their contingency to outsource a specific, and unique, Customer Requirement, to a specialist firm.

3 **Staff welfare:** Departmental and Team budgets are planned around ensuring delivery of the Customer Requirements, while maintaining a sustainable workload for each Team. From a budget planning perspective, it can help to visualise your Agile Team as a pipeline, as shown in Figure 48. The width of the pipe is your Team size, and the length is the time available to deliver. If a new, high priority, Requirement comes into the pipe, and as an Agile Team this is encouraged, the lowest priority Requirement will fall out the end. In Agile terms, the Velocity of each Team doesn't change just because you give them more work. New research actually suggests that sustained overtime can lead to a significant reduction in productivity[1,2,3,4]. If your Customer wants you to deliver the new Requirement, as well as all the older Requirements, then the pipe will need to be

---

1 *Better Work Discussion*, Seo, Paper Series No. 2 (2011).

2 *Overtime Work and Incident Coronary Heart Disease: the Whitehall II Prospective Cohort Study*, Virtanen, et al (2010).

3 *Effect of Overtime Work on Cognitive Function in Automotive Workers*, Proctor, et al (1996).

4 *Effects of Workload and 8- Versus 12-h Workday Duration on Test Battery Performance*, MacDonald and Bendak (2000).

widened (new staff added), or lengthened (additional time given), both of which will have an impact on the quote and/or budget for the Customer.

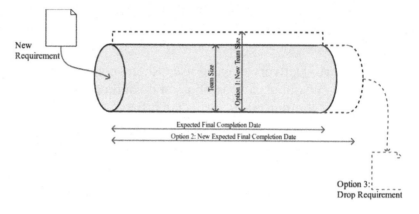

Figure 48: Team pipeline

Remember Agile principle #8: Agile processes promote sustainable development. The sponsors, developers [Team Members], and users, should be able to maintain a constant pace indefinitely.

Whilst the above changes are recommended, funding models are often outside of the Team, Department, or even organisation's control. In those cases, traditional funding models can be effective, provided there is some flexibility to adapt to changing circumstances.

Regardless of the funding models, legislative and commercial disclosure rules will always apply, whether to shareholders, government regulators, or other stakeholders. Being an Agile organisation, the financial controls for each Team or Department must promote probity, integrity, and financial transparency. A transparent financial system will streamline both internal and independent audits, and reduce the impact on operational Teams. This will also simplify the development of operational budgets, balance sheets, profit and loss statements, etc.

Quoting for Customers

'There are so many men who can figure costs, and so few who can measure values.'

Anonymous

Most Customers, regardless of whether they are internal or external, will ask the same questions. As an Agile Manager, your answers may look something like this:

'How much is this going to cost?' – 'As much as you're willing to spend.'

'How long is this going to take?' – 'As long as it takes to deliver what you ask.'

'What am I going to get?' – 'Whatever you tell us you want.'

Because of the regular Releases, and a constantly changing set of Requirements, it is best to quote Agile work under a time and materials model. This is where work will continue, until your Customer is satisfied, and stops funding the Team, without a fixed end date. Unfortunately, this funding model is not always possible, or appropriate, especially when there is significant capital costs associated with the Requirements. In these situations, providing fixed quotes is possible, but needs careful attention, to ensure they are accurate.

5: The Agile Budget

Fixed cost

Where your Customer asks for a fixed price quote, prior to agreeing work commencement, but is flexible on the scope of delivery, and how long it takes.

How to quote: Identify, and estimate, the approximate Requirements, as per *Chapter 4: Work, the Agile Way.* Use this to calculate the cost to deliver.

How to deliver:

- Work in absolute Customer priority order. Reducing the time spent on technical support Tasks will help meet short-term budget constraints, at the cost of long-term efficiency.

- Monitor Velocity and burn rate, as these are your key indicators of cost.

- For Incremental Delivery, release in short (one-two week) Iterations. Longer Iterations have a tendency to cost overruns, similar to waterfall projects.

 Example fixed cost scenario:

Customer: External Not-For-Profit Customer

Team: Production and Operations/Delivery Team

Requirement: As an office worker in the Customer's organisation/I need our office support managed/So that I can focus on my core responsibilities.

Work: Supply administration support services for a not-for-profit external client, with significant budgetary constraints.

Fixed time

Where your Customer asks for final delivery by a specific date, but is flexible in scope and cost.

How to estimate: Using historical Velocity data, each Team can estimate how many Story Points they can deliver by the due date.

How to deliver:

- For Requirements with equivalent priorities, work in Story Point order (from smallest to largest). This increases the total number of Requirements the Team can complete by the due date.

- Enforce Iteration duration for Incremental Delivery. The duration is defined by a fixed number of Iterations, and extending an Iteration will push out your final date.

Example fixed time scenario:

Customer: Sales and Marketing

Team: Media and Communications

Requirement: As a marketing manager/I need marketing material with our new corporate branding/So that I can ensure a consistent message to our external Customers.

Work: Design, and print, new marketing material for a product launch.

Fixed scope

Where your Customer has a fixed set of Requirements, but is flexible in the time it takes to deliver, and the cost of delivery. This is sometimes known as 'heavy Agile'.

How to plan: Focus on Requirements Backlog definition and estimation before commencing any Requirement, to ensure accurate scope definition.

How to deliver:

- Work in predefined, and agreed, Requirements Backlog priority order.

 Example fixed scope scenario:

Customer: External Customer

Team: Finance and Accounting

Requirement: As a small business owner/I need my annual tax return completed/So that I can fulfil my requirements to the taxation office.

Work: Complete annual tax returns in-line with legislative requirements.

Fixed cost and time

This is where your Customer asks for a fixed price quote, with final delivery due by a specified date. In this situation, the exact set of features, or scope, is flexible.

How to quote and estimate: Calculate total cost as cost per week, or cost per Iteration.

How to deliver:

- See Fixed Cost
- See Fixed Time
- Update Requirements Backlog as required.

Example fixed cost and time scenario:

Customer: External Customer

Team: Production and Operations/Delivery Team

Requirement: As a SRO/I need contracted three project managers/So that our new projects are managed in-line with industry best practices.

Work: Supply agreed services by the end of the financial year.

Fixed cost and scope

This is where your Customer asks for a fixed price quote, for a pre-defined set of Requirements. In this situation, the final date for delivery is flexible.

How to quote and plan: Increase the estimate risk during planning, to ensure your quote allows for unexpected delays that would affect your cost to deliver.

How to deliver:

- See Fixed Cost
- See Fixed Scope
- Update delivery date as required.

 Example fixed cost and scope scenario:

Customer: External Customer

Team: Production and Operations/Delivery Team

Requirement: As a building site manager/I need 13x pre-cast concrete slabs, based on our architect's designs/So that we can construct the landscape of a new building.

Work: Build and deliver to architectural specifications.

Fixed time and scope

This is where your Customer asks for a fixed set of Requirements, with final delivery due by a specified date. In this situation, the total cost to the Customer is flexible.

How to estimate and plan: Pre-assign Requirements by week, or Iteration, during planning, to define the scope delivery timetable. Pad the schedule with extra time, to cater for unexpected defects, or technical debt.

How to deliver:

- See Fixed Time
- See Fixed Scope
- Increase the size of the Team prior to completing all the Requirements (e.g. three-four Iterations for Incremental Delivery), if required, to ensure the scope is completed on time.

 Example fixed time and scope scenario:

Customer: Product and Operations Manager

Team: Human Resources Team

Requirement: As a Team/We need two new graphic designers, with mobile design skills/So that we can deliver our Customers' Requirements.

Work: Recruit required staff prior to a new project commencing.

Fixed cost, time and scope

In this final scenario, your Customer gives you no flexibility in the Requirements, from budget, schedule, or scope.

Cancel the work. This is not suitable for Agile, and should be run using a traditional framework. However, even then it is likely to fail, without some flexibility.

CHAPTER 6: REFLECTION, RETROSPECTIVES AND KAIZEN

Q 'I shall try to correct errors when shown to be errors, and I shall adopt new views so fast as they appear to be true views.'

Abraham Lincoln, 1862

Aim of this chapter: To understand Kaizen, and provide the mechanism that drives process change and corporate transformations. We investigate the Teams responsibility, as well as the specific techniques, to drive local change and support organisational change. By the end of this chapter, you should have an understanding of the processes you can use to run an Agile Business Management transformation.

All Agile processes are, by their very nature, cyclical, with the outcomes of the previous Iteration feeding into the next. With very little additional effort, this continuous feedback can become ongoing improvement, and provide the mechanism for organisations to adapt to changing circumstances. This *process of continuous improvement*, or Kaizen[1], leads to a *culture of continuous improvement*.

All processes and business functions within your organisation, are candidates for Kaizen, and are everyone's responsibility, from the CEO to the newest Team Member. In addition to productivity improvement, Kaizen needs to address efficiencies in other areas, such as organisational

---

1 *Kaizen (Ky'zen), The Key to Japan's Competitive Success*, Imai (1986).

culture, staff morale, communication and management, as a form of total quality management[2].

There are five main elements to Kaizen:

1 **Teamwork:** All staff, regardless of rank or status, work together towards the common goals of your organisation. By extension, all staff, across every Team, need to understand the implications of their work for the rest of the organisation, and share the responsibility for your organisation's success.

2 **Personal discipline:** Staff should be accountable for their actions. Not only for their core responsibilities, but for all aspects of their work, including quality control, time management, financial management, and their professional relationships with colleagues and Customers. There is a corresponding requirement for organisations to set reasonable standards, and challenge staff to meet them.

3 **Improved morale:** As covered in *Chapter 1: You, the Agile* Manager, you are responsible for creating a supportive environment where staff feel empowered, secure, and have a sense of ownership. An organisation with low morale, or conflict between managers and staff, will suffer from high absenteeism, poor engagement, and reduced productivity.

4 **Quality circles/Retrospective workshop:** The retrospective workshops are the primary forum for Teams to suggest improvements to your corporate culture, delivery processes and management arrangements. You should also encourage cross-Team

---

2 *BS 7850-1: Total Quality Management. Guide to Management Principles*, British Standards Institution (1992).

retrospectives, as a means to share ideas, skills and technology improvements. You need to ensure Teams have the authority to experiment with, and implement, local changes, while your organisation should be quick to respond to any large-scale suggestions that have implications beyond the Team.

5 **Suggestions for improvement:** All business functions are candidates for Kaizen, and, as such, each Team Member has an obligation to participate in the continuous improvement process. Learning, observing, and putting forward new ideas, especially in relation to their core responsibilities, will help remove any impediments, and increase work efficiency. As an Agile manager, you are responsible for creating a culture in which your staff feel empowered to make these suggestions.

Kaizen is a truly continuous process, where Teams should be seeking new ways of improving the business every day. Staff should be encouraged to experiment with different process changes, to drive continuous improvement. However, you should teach your staff the scientific method, to ensure effective and low-risk experimentation. The five steps to this method are; create a hypothesis, design an experiment, run the experiment, draw conclusions, and communicate the results.

The regular, Retrospective workshop, provides a forum for each of your Teams for introspection, and reflection on the management processes that support the day-to-day operation. Figure 49 shows a simple retrospective feedback cycle.

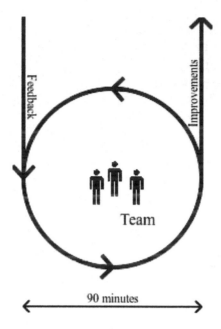

Figure 49: Retrospective cycle

Each Team holds a regular (weekly, biweekly, or at the end of each Iteration), Retrospective workshop, to discuss the management and delivery processes. The goal of this workshop is to suggest improvements, and the focus should be, in order of importance, people, relationships, process, and tools. The full Team should be present for each Retrospective, as they are responsible, and accountable, for driving process improvements in the organisation, and their Team.

Remember Agile principle #12: At regular intervals, the Team reflects on how to become more effective, then tunes, and adjusts, its behaviour accordingly.

Teams should be free to discuss any relevant topic. During this short meeting, between an hour to half a day, the Team should reflect on the processes since the last Retrospective. This may include:

- Discuss the processes that worked well, and were effective, or improved, since the last Retrospective. By reflecting on the positive outcomes, the Team can identify their strengths, and use those to overcome specific weaknesses. It is also important, as a mechanism, to provide positive feedback to the Team.

- Discuss the processes that did not work as well as expected, and need improvement. By reflecting on the negative outcomes, the Team can focus their effort on improving in that area, or make modifications to the process to better play to their strengths.

- Suggest any specific improvements to the processes used within the Team. As mentioned, continuous improvement (Kaizen) is a core concept to Agile and Agile Business Management, and the Team is responsible for driving most of this change. It is important to ensure that each improvement is actionable, and assigned an owner.

> As the presence of managers can sometimes stifle free and unfettered conversation, you may want to provide opportunities for your Teams to run some retrospectives without you.

Topics available for consideration include; Team structure, communication, meeting arrangements, tools and automation, process definitions, as well as the delivery mechanisms. At the end of the Retrospective, the Team should have a list of 'assigned' and 'actionable' improvements to the management processes.

Each Retrospective provides the Team with the opportunity to reflect on the time since the last Retrospective, and drive continuous process improvement out of any learning's since then. Through this process of Kaizen, the delivery of each Requirement should be more effective, and enjoyable, than the last.

CHAPTER 7: THE SHAPE OF THINGS TO COME

> 'Imagination is more important than knowledge. For knowledge is limited, whereas imagination embraces the entire world, stimulating progress, giving birth to evolution.'
>
> Albert Einstein, 1931

As I said at the beginning of this book, Agile is about change; changing how you think, changing how you work, and changing the way you interact. Agile Business Management provides the guiding philosophy and supporting processes to help catalyse this change within your organisation. How you apply this is between you, your Teams, and your Customers.

Whatever your ultimate goals, an Agile organisation emphasises adaptability and Customer interaction, while remaining aligned to the four core Agile values.

1 We value **individuals and interactions** over processes and tools.

2 We value **[completed Customer Requirements]** over comprehensive documentation.

3 We value **customer collaboration** over contract negotiation.

4 We value **responding to change** over following a plan.

These values form the foundation, and Agile Business Management provides the framework to build your organisation. You need to take that foundation and framework, and build the rest.

In these last few pages, let's look at the first steps that you may take as part of an Agile Business Management transformation. I must caveat that this is an example transformation. Your organisational culture, strengths, weaknesses, and priorities, will drive the steps that you take. For instance, I have worked with several Asian organisations where title, and rank, was very important to staff. During these transformations, we retained much of the existing structure and related titles, while mapping these to Agile responsibilities.

A final thought before we drill into the example transformation. Out of all the techniques, processes and philosophies in Agile, never underestimate the importance of common sense.

Pre-Agile › Learning Agile

Where do you start with something as complex as an organisational transformation? I'd recommend you start with a vision, and a short business case, defining the expected end state, and core benefits you hope to achieve. Remember that this is Agile, and your vision and goal, can, and will, change throughout the life of the transformation. Defining outcomes and benefits is only half the story, you also need to define the organisational maturity measures that you will use to validate progress and benefits realisation.

If you haven't done so already, you need to engage with the rest of your organisation. Workshops, and one-on-one meetings with Teams, are a good way to make sure everyone understands the new values of the organisation. This engagement process should encourage a culture of transparency, and drive the change from a process-driven organisation, to a relationship-driven organisation.

Throughout this engagement, you also need to ensure that new staff understand the Agile corporate goals. This stage of the transformation programme is the perfect opportunity to develop an Agile recruitment policy, to ensure new employees understand the Agile approach, and will fit into the new organisational culture.

Next, is to put in place the mechanism to review, and drive, iterative change throughout the organisation – the Retrospective workshop. This is also a good time to introduce Agile Meeting processes, to facilitate efficient Retrospectives, workshops, and other internal business meetings.

With the Retrospectives in place, it becomes easier to transition to smaller, and more frequent, deliverables. You can also begin to design, and map, workflow processes for some of your Teams and Departments, and transition them to Continuous, or Incremental, Delivery processes. Some Teams will have complex workflow and delivery processes, and you can transition these in at a later stage. Finally, you can't have Continuous or Incremental Delivery without appropriate planning and design, so you also need to introduce Agile planning sessions.

You should begin to put in place Kanban Boards, to track, and visualise, and control the workflow of those Teams that you have transitioned. You can create an initial, best guess, WIP limit, and optimise it later. Though it may be difficult for your Teams, starting with low WIP limits will help identify bottlenecks, and other constraints.

Towards the end of this initial transformation phase, you will want to begin the organisational restructure process. It will take a long time to define the areas of responsibility, and the boundaries between departments, and even longer to engage all of the staff in the restructure process. Begin the process of restructuring by sharing resources and skills within the existing structure, to create functional Cross-Functional Teams.

Alongside each of these process, value and mindset, changes, is the continuous, and targeted, coaching of managers, staff, and Customers alike. Managers need to learn new ways of engaging with their Teams, as well as understanding the new organisational performance measures. Departmental staff need appropriate training, to ensure a smooth transition to their new processes and responsibilities. Finally, Customers, both internal and external, need to learn how their role and responsibilities will change under the new management processes.

Early Agile › Agile management

Depending on the size of your organisation, the previous stage of this example transformation could take upwards of 12 months. However, once your organisation has settled into simple, Agile processes, and there is an overall understanding of the values, and goals of Agile, across all staff and Customers, we can begin to push the transformation to the next stage.

In this stage, we can begin to invest in overarching Agile governance. Introducing Agile executive governance bodies, such as the investment committee, information management committee, or project steering committees, will bring strong governance to the organisation, in line with core Agile principles. With Agile governance structures in place, create Agile KPIs, to measure the performance of managers and executives against the Agile goals of the organisation.

It also makes sense to transition existing management processes to Agile, such as financial management, or business case policies. Establish new delegation and contingency rules to provide a level of autonomy at a Team level. Allow decisions based on short, concise, business cases, with the understanding that things will change. Finally, if possible, change the organisation's budgeting process to an iterative model, to take advantage of emerging opportunities.

Required governance processes, should be integrated into the new Agile processes. Depending on your industry, or Customer demands, processes, such as CMMI, ISO20000, or ISO38500, can co-exist with Agile Business Management. Of course, as with all business transformations, apply common sense to your decisions.

As the organisational restructure continues, this is a good opportunity to introduce Self-Organising Teams, while ensuring that existing business functions continue to operate.

I would usually take this opportunity to undertake an external Customer audit. This audit would review the trust levels, relationships, and interaction between each Customer and the organisation. From here, I would begin to transition each Customer, starting with the closest relationships, to take on their new Agile responsibilities. This includes building, and maintaining, the Requirement Backlog, working closely with the Team during each stage of delivery, and participating in Team planning and review meetings.

As Teams and their Customers begin to integrate, I would supplement their existing training with communications training. Given how quickly Requirements can change, communication skills become critically important. Misunderstandings can quickly spiral out of control, and can break the bond between the Team and Customer, if they aren't identified, and resolved, early.

There needs to be an ongoing refinement of the processes and strategies implemented during the first stage. Through the Retrospectives, each Team should review their processes to identify bottlenecks, constraints and optimisations. This should lead to adjustments in workflow states, processes, and WIP Limits, as well as improvements to Team communication, and collaboration with their Customers. If Teams haven't already implemented them, they should begin to measure, and visualise, progress against plans, with burndown charts, cumulative flow diagrams, and run charts, as appropriate.

Finally, once you have good management, you can begin to investigate supporting tools, to simplify many of your new Agile processes. Investing in workflow (Kanban) and Backlog management tools, can simplify the administration, and visualisation, of Customer Requirements, while communication tools, such as video conferencing systems, can improve overall interaction across multiple sites and Teams.

7: The Shape of Things to Come

Agile practitioners › Continuous improvement

With good Agile management in place, we can begin the final stage of our example Agile transformation; reinforcing cultural change, and driving continuous process improvement across the organisation.

You should have completed the formal organisational restructure at this point. The design of departments, and business functions, should be around the efficient delivery of Customer Requirements. There will almost certainly be further changes to meet evolving organisational needs, but you should have a lean management hierarchy, with delegated authority to cross-functional and empowered Teams. As with all restructures, this may lead to redundancies, if positions become surplus to requirements, or people are unwilling, or unable, to adapt to their new roles. However, given the transparent nature of Agile, the rationale behind the redundancies should be evident to all staff.

Self-organising Teams need to have an awareness of the skills available within the organisation. Ideally, Teams should achieve this through open communication between themselves, but, for very large organisations, you may undertake a formal skills audit. The organisational structure should include Centres of Excellence (or Competency Centres), to facilitate the development, and management, of specific organisational skills.

If not already addressed, review, and formalise, quality control and quality assurance processes within each Department, business function and Team. Where possible, encourage Teams to utilise Test-Driven Work, by defining quality control measures and tests upfront, prior to beginning any work.

Teams should continuously review, and refine, their workflow processes, to resolve any new bottlenecks and constraints. Teams should also begin to take on new responsibilities for risk management, and corporate strategy.

With an understanding of their workflow, Teams can begin to utilise formal estimation techniques, to improve their Requirement (or Iteration) planning. Accompany estimates with appropriate measures, visualisation, and regular reviews, to improve the overall accuracy of the process. However, as with the introduction of all new processes, measure the performance of the Team, to ensure that the new process actually produces a net positive impact.

Finally, you can begin to investigate the specific benefits to your organisation of some of the more controversial Agile, and Agile Business Management techniques, such as Pair Work, monthly budgeting, and time-based estimation.

Remember that this is a process of continuous improvement, that there is no end. You don't have a Gantt chart on your wall showing when your Agile transformation is complete. Where there is benefit, and the value of that benefit outweighs the cost, there is change, and there is Agile.

The next step in the Agile journey is yours to take.

GLOSSARY

Term	Definition
Acceptance Testing	See User Acceptance Testing.
Active (Kanban)	State: Tasks that are actively being worked on by a Team Member.
Actual Hours	The total effort to Complete a Task, or Requirement, as measured when complete.
Agile	A generic term that describes over 50, sometimes conflicting, methods and frameworks for working in an adaptable, Customer focused, and Incremental way.
Agile Business Management	A series of concepts and processes for the day-to-day management of your organisation, regardless of industry, size, or location. The end goal is to improve quality, business adaptability, staff engagement, and risk management, for the benefit of your Customers.
Agile Manager	A corporate leader who embodies the principles and values of Agile.
Assignee	The Team Member responsible for delivering a Task or Requirement.
Automated Quality Control Test	A Quality Control Test that can be run, regularly, without human interaction.

Automated Unit Test	See Automated Quality Control Test.
Backlog	See Requirements Backlog.
BAU	See Business-as-usual.
Blocked (Kanban)	State: Tasks that have upstream, or downstream, dependencies, external to the Team, that are preventing progress.
Burndown Chart	A visualisation of the total effort, and effort remaining, against time.
Burnup Chart	A visualisation of the total effort, and effort remaining in the Requirements Backlog, against time.
Business Area	See Department.
Business Function	See Department.
Business Team	See Department.
Business Unit	See Department.
Business-as-usual	The standard, ongoing, work, undertaken by a Business Team.
Card (Kanban)	A visualisation of a Task (or Requirement).
Card Wall	See Kanban Board.
Centres of Excellence	A shared internal Team that provides governance, and support, on specific technologies, processes, and business areas.
Committed Parties	Stakeholders, and Team Members, who are actively working towards delivering Requirements for the Customer.
Competency Centres	See Centres of Excellence.

Complete	See Done.
Consumer	An individual or organisation that purchases products, or services, from you, but does not have any authority, or responsibility, in the design, and development, of the product/service.
Continuous Delivery	Planning and delivering related, or unrelated, Requirements, as they are identified and prioritised.
Continuous Improvement	See Kaizen.
Control Limit	The bounds of expected variance within the Team's processes. Processes that exceed this control limit can be said to be uncontrolled.
Cross-Functional	Where individuals with different, and complementary, skills work together as a Team.
Cumulative Flow Diagram	A visualisation of the elapsed time, and number of Tasks, or Requirements, remaining in each state, against time.
Customer	An individual (or organisation) who engages one or more Teams, to deliver a series of Requirements, and who has the responsibility, and authority, to direct the delivery of the products or services.
Customer Representative	An individual delegated with the authority to act on behalf of the Customer.
Customer Requirement	See Requirement.

Cycle Time	The time taken between starting, and completing, work on a Requirement.
Cycle Time Run Chart	A visualisation of the Cycle Time (or Lead Time), compared with the average Cycle Time and bounded by the expected tolerances.
Daily Scrum	See Daily Stand-up.
Daily Stand-up	A daily, 15 minute, Team meeting, to discuss progress, plans and issues.
Defect	A shortcoming, imperfection, or lack, in an otherwise completed Requirement.
Deliverable	The product, or service, created by the Team (or Teams), to fulfil a specific Requirement. Each Deliverable generally only fulfils a single Requirement, so a large project may consist of many Deliverables.
Delivery Teams	An internal Department responsible for building core products, and/or, delivering core services. Due to the highly variable range of responsibilities for Production and Operations Teams between organisations, Agile Business Management simplifies this by calling them all 'Delivery Teams'.

Department	A specific group within your organisation, responsible for a specific business function, subject area, service, or product. Human Resources, Finance and Accounting, and Sales and Marketing, are all examples of Departments. Departments may also be known as Groups, Divisions, Organisation Units, or Business Areas.
Do	The process of actively working on the Requirements.
Done (Kanban)	State: Tasks that are complete, and ready to be delivered to the Customer.
Driver (TDD)	Pair Work: Responsible for doing the work, be that writing, developing, building, etc.
Effort	Only the specific time required to complete a Task or Requirement, excluding any overhead.
Estimate	The process of calculating the effort required to deliver a Requirement.
Expedite (Kanban)	A high-priority track for urgent Requirements and Tasks.
Extreme Programming	An Agile software engineering framework.
Feature Driven Development	An Agile design and development framework, supporting the planning, design, and building of large-scale projects.

Finance and Accounting	An internal department responsible for managing all the financial and monetary aspects of the business.
Governance	Consistent management, cohesive policies, guidance, processes and decision-rights, for a given area of responsibility.
HR	See Human Resources.
Human Resources	An internal department responsible for staff recruitment and management policies.
ICT Support	An internal department responsible for the day-to-day administration of IT assets.
In Progress (Kanban)	A sub-state, within Kanban, for Tasks that are currently being worked on by any member of the Team.
Incremental Delivery	Planning, and delivering, related Requirements in short, fixed-time blocks.
Involved Parties	Stakeholders who have an interest in the outcome, but are not responsible for day-to-day delivery.
Issue	An issue is an event, change, or risk, that has occurred, or is occurring.
Iteration	A repeating timebox of fixed duration, allocated to the delivery of one or more Requirements, from a larger piece of work.
Iteration Backlog	An ordered list of Tasks to be delivered during an Iteration.

Iteration Burndown Chart	See Burndown Chart.
Iteration Retrospective	See Retrospective.
Iteration Velocity	See Velocity.
JIT	See Just-In-Time.
Just-In-Time	A production strategy that strives to improve a business return on investment, by reducing waiting inventory, and associated carrying costs.
Kaizen	A philosophy, culture and technique of driving continuous improvement in work processes and business functions.
Kanban	A lean, continuous workflow management and improvement process.
Kanban Board	A tool to visualise, and control, the workflow of Tasks and Requirements.
Kanban Card	See Card.
Key Performance Indicator	A performance measurement to evaluate the success of a particular activity.
KPI	See Key Performance Indicator.
Lead Time	The time taken between adding a Requirement to the Requirements Backlog, and releasing it to the Customer.
Lead Time Run Chart	See Cycle Time Run Chart.

Lower Control Limit	See Control Limit.
Media and Communications	An internal department responsible for interacting with the public, media press releases, brand awareness, and occasionally, social media.
Minimal Marketable Feature	See Requirement.
Not Done	Requirements that are incomplete at the end of an Iteration.
Observer (TDD)	Pair Work: Responsible for advising, and reviewing, the work.
Organisation Unit	See Department.
Outcome	See Requirement.
Pair Programming (XP)	See Pair Work.
Pair Work	A technique in which each Team Member works as part of a pair, at a single workstation, as either a 'Driver' or 'Observer'.
Planning	The process of determining the target scope of delivery, and (if appropriate) defining the Iteration Backlog.
Planning Poker	An estimation game that promotes collaboration and consensus building during the estimation process.
Product Backlog (Scrum)	See Requirements Backlog.
Product Owner (Scrum)	See Customer Representative.

Production and Operations	See Delivery Teams.
Project	See Requirement.
QA	See Quality Assurance.
Quality Assurance	The process of improving development and test processes, to increase overall quality, and reduce defects.
Quality Control	The act of identifying defects by testing, validating, and verifying a completed product, or service, against the Customers' Requirements.
Quality Control Test	A formal procedure that identifies potential defects by examining the specific output of a Deliverable.
R&D	See Research and Development.
Ready (Kanban)	A sub-state within Kanban, for Tasks that are waiting to move to the next state.
Release	The process of delivering completed Requirements to the Customer.
Release Burnup Chart	See Burnup Chart.
Requirement	Also called a User Story, or Minimal Marketable Feature, a Requirement is a specific, documented, and Deliverable, Customer need.
Requirements Backlog	An ordered list of Requirements; maintained by the Customer, and estimated by the Team.

Research and Development	An internal department responsible for improving existing products and services, as well as creating new ones.
Retrospective	A regular Team meeting to review, and reflect on, the management processes that support the day-to-day operation.
Review	The (formal or informal) process of verifying that the completed Requirement meets the Customer's expectations, and accepting them for Release.
Risk	A risk is something (generally negative) that could happen, and is assessed in terms of likelihood and potential impact.
Risk Register	A log of all risks for a specific Team and Customer.
Sales and Marketing	An internal Department responsible for the promotion, pricing, market research, and the sale of your products and services.
Scrum	An Agile project and product management framework (*www.scrum.org*).
Scrum Master (Scrum)	See Team Facilitator.
Scrum of Scrums (Scrum)	See Summary Stand-up.

Self-Organising	The responsibility of the Team to create a functional, internal Team structure, by replacing, and reorganising, Team Members as needed.
Sign-off	The formal approval that a Requirement has been completed to the Customer's satisfaction.
Sprint (Scrum)	See Iteration.
Sprint Backlog (Scrum)	See Iteration Backlog.
Sprint Retrospective (Scrum)	See Retrospective.
Sprint Velocity (Scrum)	See Velocity.
Staff Overhead	Any time used by a staff member during working hours, not in the delivery of Tasks or Requirements. Overhead includes; breaks, meetings, illness, and assisting other Team Members.
Story	See Requirement.
Story Point	An arbitrary number intended to represent all of the effort required for the whole Team to complete a single Requirement, relative to a reference Requirement.
Summary Stand-up	A Daily Stand-up consisting of representatives from each of the Teams, with a Department or project.

Task	A discrete activity that forms a subset of a Requirement. Put another way, the delivery of each Requirement requires the delivery of one or more Tasks.
TDD	See Test-Driven Work.
TDW	See Test-Driven Work.
Team	A small group of between five and nine staff, containing a cross-section of skills, permanently, or temporarily, grouped together to deliver one or more Customer's Requirements.
Team Facilitator	The person responsible for managing the Agile process within a Team. The Team Facilitator can be a Team leader or Team Member.
Technical Debt	Technical 'Requirements' in the Requirements Backlog that are not directly requests from the Customers, but are needed to improve overall quality of the product or service.
Test	See Quality Control Test.
Test-Driven Development	An Agile quality management process. Also, see Test-Driven Work.
Test-Driven Work	The act of writing Quality Control Tests prior to beginning any work, rather than after.
Testing (Kanban)	State: Tasks that are functionally Done, but undergoing formal validation to verify the Task was completed successfully.

Glossary

Timebox	A fixed period of time allocated to an activity, or specific event.
Unit Test	See Automated Quality Control Test.
Upper Control Limit	See Control Limit.
User Acceptance Testing	A series of quality assurance tests undertaken by the Customer, to ensure that the Deliverable meets their Requirements and expectations.
User Story	See Requirement.
Velocity	The rate of delivery of Requirements per Iteration, or other fixed period.
Vision	A brief description of the expected end state after the Team completes all the Customer Requirements. This will change as the Customer Requirements change.
WIP Limit (Kanban)	See Work In Progress.
Work	The sum of Requirements made by a single Customer to a Team, or related group of Teams, and delivered in an Incremental, or Continuous, manner.
Work In Progress Limit (Kanban)	A limit on a Kanban column (or state) to identify, and control, bottlenecks and process limitations.
Work Package	See Requirement.
Working Hours	The total time a Team Member spends at work (usually between seven and a half, and eight hours per day).

BIBLIOGRAPHY

Anderson, David J. *Kanban: Successful Evolutionary Change for Your Technology Business.* Blue Hole Press, 2010.

Arisholm, Erik, Hans Gallis, Tore Dyba, and Dag Sjoberg. "Evaluating Pair Programming with Respect to System Complexity and Programmer Expertise." *IEEE Transactions on Software Engineering*, Feb 2007.

Beck, Kent. *Extreme Programming Explained: Embrace Change.* Addison-Wesley, 1999.

—. *Test-Driven Development by Example.* Addison-Wesley, 2003.

Beedle, Mike, et al. *Agile Manifesto.* n.d. *http://agilemanifesto.org/*.

Boyd, Colonel John. *The Essence of Winning and Losing.* n.d. *www.danford.net/boyd/essence.htm*.

British Standards Institution. "BS 7850-1: Total quality management. Guide to management principles." 1992.

Carnegie Mellon University; Software Engineering Institute. *Capability Maturity Model Integration.* n.d. *www.sei.cmu.edu/cmmi/*.

Cockburn, Alistair, and Laurie Williams. "The Costs and Benefits of Pair Programming." *Proceedings of the First International Conference on Extreme Programming and Flexible Processes in Software Engineering (XP2000)*, 2000.

Cohn, Mike. *Agile Estimating and Planning.* Prentice Hall, 2005.

Bibliography

De Feo, Joseph, and William Barnard. *JURAN Institute's Six Sigma Breakthrough and Beyond - Quality Performance Breakthrough Methods.* Tata McGraw-Hill Publishing, 2005.

De Luca, J, P Coad, and E Lefebvre. *Java Modeling In Color With UML: Enterprise Components and Process.* Prentice Hall International, 1999.

DeMarco, Tom, and Timothy Lister. *Waltzing With Bears: Managing Risk on Software Projects.* Dorset House, 2003.

Deming, W. Edwards. *Out of the Crisis.* Massachusetts Institute of Technology, 1982.

—. *The New Economics for Industry, Government, Education.* Massachusetts Institute of Technology, 1993.

Dennis, Pascal. *Lean Production Simplified.* Productivity Press, 2007.

Evans, James, and William Lindsay. *The Management and Control of Quality.* South-Western, 2008.

Fowler, Martin, and Kent Beck. *Refactoring: Improving the Design of Existing Code.* Addison-Wesley Professional, 1999.

Glazer, Hillel. "Love and Marriage: CMMI and Agile Need Each Other." *CROSSTALK: The Journal of Defense Software Engineering,* Jan/Feb 2010.

Glazer, Hillel, Jeff Dalton, David Anderson, Mike Konrad, and Sandy Shrum. *CMMI® or Agile: Why Not Embrace Both!* Software Engineering Institute, 2008.

Goldratt, Eliyahu M, and Jeff Cox. *The goal: a process of ongoing improvement.* 1986.

Grenning, James. "Planning Poker or How to avoid analysis paralysis while release planning." 2002.

Bibliography

Imai, Masaaki. *Kaizen: The Key To Japan's Competitive Success.* McGraw-Hill, 1986.

Johnson, Brian, and John Higgins. *Software Lifecycle; practical strategy and design principle.* Van Haren Publishing, 2007.

Johnson, Brian, and Richard Warden. *Software Lifecycle Support.* H.M. Stationery Office, 1993.

Kaplan, Robert, and David P. Norton. *The Balanced Scorecard: Translating Strategy Into Action.* Harvard Business Press, 1996.

Kirkpatrick, Doug. *Beyond Empowerment: The Age of the Self-Managed Organization.* 2011.

Lu, David John, and Nihon Nōritsu Kyōkai. *Kanban Just-in Time at Toyota: Management Begins at the Workplace.* Productivity Press, 1986.

Lui, Kim Man, Keith Chan, and John Nosek. "The Effect of Pairs in Program Design Tasks." *IEEE Transactions on Software Engineering,* Feb 2008.

MacDonald, W., and S. Bendak. "Effects of workload and 8- versus 12-h workday duration on test battery performance." *International Journal of Industrial Ergonomics,* 2000.

Male, Mack D. *Transforming the City of Edmonton IT Branch.* 2009. *http://blog.mastermaq.ca/2009/07/02/transforming-the-city-of-edmonton-it-branch/.*

Maslow, Abraham. *Motivation and Personality.* Harper and Row Publishers, 1987.

Ohno, Taiichi. *Toyota Production System: Beyond Large-Scale Production.* Productivity Press, 1988.

Organisation for Economic Co-operation and Development. *OECD Principles of Corporate Governance.* OECD Publications Service, 2004.

Bibliography

Palmer, S.R, and J.M Felsing. *A Practical Guide to Feature-Driven Development.* Prentice Hall, 2002.

Paulk, Mark C. "Extreme Programming from a CMM Perspective." *IEEE SOFTWARE,* Nov/Dec 2001.

Proctor, S. P., R. F. White, T. G. Robins, D. Echeverria, and A. Z. Rocskay. "Effect of overtime work on cognitive function in automotive workers." *Scandinavian Journal of Work, Environment and Health,* 1996.

Schwaber, Ken, and Jeff Sutherland. *Scrum Guide.* Scrum.org, 2011.

Schwaber, Ken, and Mike Beedle. *Agile software development with Scrum.* Prentice Hall, 2002.

Scrum Alliance. *Scrum.* n.d. http://scrum.org/.

Seo, Ji-Won. *Better Work Discussion Paper Series No. 2.* International Labour Organisation, 2011.

Socha, David, Tyler C. Folsom, and Joe Justice. "Applying Agile Software Principles and Practices for Fast Automotive Development." *Proceedings of the FISITA 2012 World Automotive Congress, Lecture Notes in Electrical Engineering Volume 196, 2013.* Springer Berlin Heidelberg, 2012. pp 1033-1045.

Sutherland, Jeffrey, and Ken Schwaber. "Business object design and implementation." *OOPSLA '95 workshop proceedings,* 1995.

Taleb, Nassim Nicholas. *The Black Swan: The Impact of the Highly Improbable.* Random House, 2007.

Virtanen, Marianna, et al. "Overtime work and incident coronary heart disease: the Whitehall II prospective cohort study." *European Heart Journal,* 2010.

Wake, Bill. *INVEST in Good Stories, and SMART Tasks.* n.d. http://xp123.com/articles/invest-in-good-stories-and-smart-tasks/.

Bibliography

Williams, Laurie, and Robert Kessler. *Pair Programming Illuminated.* Pearson Education Inc, 2003.

Womack, James P, Daniel T Jones, and Daniel Roos. *The Machine That Changed the World.* Harper Perennial, 1991.

ITG RESOURCES

IT Governance Ltd sources, creates and delivers products and services to meet the real-world, evolving IT governance needs of today's organisations, directors, managers and practitioners.

The ITG website (_www.itgovernance.co.uk_) is the international one-stop-shop for corporate and IT governance information, advice, guidance, books, tools, training and consultancy.

_www.itgovernance.co.uk/project_governance.aspx_ is the information page on our website for Agile resources.

Other Websites

Books and tools published by IT Governance Publishing (ITGP) are available from all business booksellers and are also immediately available from the following websites:

www.itgovernance.eu is our euro-denominated website which ships from Benelux and has a growing range of books in European languages other than English.

www.itgovernanceusa.com is a US$-based website that delivers the full range of IT Governance products to North America, and ships from within the continental US.

www.itgovernanceasia.com provides a selected range of ITGP products specifically for customers in the Indian sub-continent.

www.itgovernance.asia delivers the full range of ITGP publications, serving countries across Asia Pacific. Shipping from Hong Kong, US dollars, Singapore dollars, Hong Kong dollars, New Zealand dollars and Thai baht are all accepted through the website.

Toolkits

ITG's unique range of toolkits includes the IT Governance Framework Toolkit, which contains all the tools and guidance that you will need in order to develop and implement an appropriate IT governance framework for your organisation.

For a free paper on how to use the proprietary Calder-Moir IT Governance Framework, and for a free trial version of the toolkit, see *www.itgovernance.co.uk/calder_moir.aspx*.

There is also a wide range of toolkits to simplify implementation of management systems, such as an ISO/IEC 27001 ISMS or an ISO/IEC 22301 BCMS, and these can all be viewed and purchased online at *www.itgovernance.co.uk*.

Training Services

IT Governance offers an extensive portfolio of training courses designed to educate information security, IT governance, risk management and compliance professionals. Our classroom and online training programmes will help you develop the skills required to deliver best practice and compliance to your organisation. They will also enhance your career by providing you with industry standard certifications and increased peer recognition. Our range of courses offer a structured learning path from Foundation to Advanced level in the key topics of information security, IT governance, business continuity and service management.

Our *Implementing IT Governance: Foundation and Principles* training course delivers introductory training to raise awareness, build knowledge and develop a complete understanding of IT governance and its implementation. It has been specifically designed to show delegates how to create a single integrated management framework that ensures that IT truly supports and delivers on all organisational strategies and objectives.

Full details of all IT Governance training courses can be found at *www.itgovernance.co.uk/training.aspx*.

Professional Services and Consultancy

The IT Governance Professional Services team can show you how to apply Agile concepts to the most complex development projects. Our expert consultants can guide and inspire you in the use of Agile, providing you with the practical techniques to improve delivery efficiencies, control your implementation costs, and meet your sales targets by building customer loyalty.

We believe that Agile Business Management is hard work and requires a cultural shift from the traditional business practices of hierarchical corporate structures, customer engagement, staff management, and work processes. We will show you the Agile methods that create flexibility and ensure adaptability to changing circumstances, accepting that nothing changes more than your Customer's needs. You will learn how to change from a traditional hierarchy towards self-empowered individuals and Teams. In this way, you will develop engaged employees with the responsibility, accountability and authority to deliver to the Customer's Requirements, shaping and directing outcomes, while regularly delivering partial, though functional, products.

For more information about IT Governance: Consultancy and Training Services see:

www.itgovernance.co.uk/consulting.aspx.

Publishing Services

IT Governance Publishing (ITGP) is the world's leading IT-GRC publishing imprint that is wholly owned by IT Governance Ltd.

With books and tools covering all IT governance, risk and compliance frameworks, we are the publisher of choice for authors and distributors alike, producing unique and practical publications of the highest quality, in the latest formats available, which readers will find invaluable.

www.itgovernancepublishing.co.uk is the website dedicated to ITGP enabling both current and future authors, distributors, readers and other interested parties, to have easier access to more information. This allows ITGP website visitors to keep up to date with the latest publications and news.

Newsletter

IT governance is one of the hottest topics in business today, not least because it is also the fastest moving.

You can stay up to date with the latest developments across the whole spectrum of IT governance subject matter, including; risk management, information security, ITIL and IT service management, project governance, compliance and so much more, by subscribing to ITG's core publications and topic alert emails.

Simply visit our subscription centre and select your preferences: *www.itgovernance.co.uk/newsletter.aspx*.

CPSIA information can be obtained
at www.ICGtesting.com
Printed in the USA
BVOW06s1249230217
476867BV00008B/205/P